Preface

The purpose of the book is to introduce students to web application development in Java with the use of Eclipse. The book assumes a familiarity with HTML and the Java programming language.

The book is in cookbook format in that it provides instructions on how to construct solutions to various problems. The intent is to show students how to accomplish typical Web development tasks in the Java language. In later chapters of the book, detailed instructions are omitted if they duplicate instructions in an earlier chapter. This assumes the student can recall or refer back to the previous instructions. Unguided exercises are also provided so that students can apply what they have covered in the main text. The book omits many details and explanations. For these, the reader will need to consult online documentation or search the Web for other tutorials and articles. Each chapter contains a list of references that the reader may find useful for filling in these missing details.

This is an active book in the sense that the reader is expected to carry out the procedures described. The code examples provided in each chapter are not self-contained; they need to be developed by progressing sequentially through the chapters.

Acknowledgements

The following people have helped to create this book.

- Eyob Zellke
- Patrick O'Conner
- The students of Winter quarter 2008 of Server Programming at CSUSB

Contents

1 Introduction to Java Web Application Development   **11**
    1.1 Objectives 11
    1.2 Overview 11
    1.3 Computer Languages Used for Web Application Development 12
    1.4 The Servlet API 13
    1.5 Java 2 Enterprise Edition (J2EE) 13
    1.6 Java Server Pages (JSP) 14
    1.7 Rich Site Summary (RSS) 14
    1.8 Representational State Transfer (REST) 15
    1.9 Web Services 15
    1.10 Integrated Development Environments 15
    1.11 Ant 16
    1.12 Web Application Architecture 16
    1.13 Security 17
    1.14 Web Application Servers 18
    1.15 Database Servers 18
    1.16 Development versus Deployment Environments 18

2 Java Setup   **21**
    2.1 Objectives 21
    2.2 Overview 21
    2.3 Installation 21
    2.4 Exercises 22

3 Eclipse Setup   **23**
    3.1 Objectives 23
    3.2 Overview 23

3.3 Installation 24

3.4 Issues 24

3.5 Configure File Types 24

3.6 Exercises 26

4 The Apache Tomcat Web Container   **27**

4.1 Objectives 27

4.2 Overview 27

4.3 Install Tomcat 28

4.4 Test 28

4.5 Issues 28

4.6 Configure Firewall 30

4.7 Manager Application 31

4.8 Tomcat Documentation 31

4.9 Log Files 34

4.10 Understanding Tomcat Class Loading 35

4.11 Deep Restart of Tomcat 36

4.12 Exercises 36

5 Java Servlets   **39**

5.1 Objectives 39

5.2 Overview 39

5.3 Project Creation 40

5.4 Attaching Source Code to Jar Files 41

5.5 Deployment Descriptor 45

5.6 Create Home Servlet 47

5.7 Web Application Deployment 54

5.8 Exercises 55

6 Web Application Logging   **57**

6.1 Objectives 57

6.2 Overview 57

6.3 Add the Log4j Library to the Project 58

6.4 The Log4j Configuration File 60

6.5 The Eclipse Build Process 60

6.6 Modify HomeServlet 61

6.7 Exercises 64

7 Java Server Pages **65**

7.1 Objectives 65

7.2 References 65

7.3 Overview 65

7.4 Create a JSP 69

7.5 Exercises 74

8 A Simple News Feed Application **77**

8.1 Objectives 77

8.2 References 77

8.3 Overview 77

8.4 Flow of information for RSS 78

8.5 Install Libraries 79

8.6 Modify the JSP 83

8.7 Test 84

8.8 Create Publisher Project 84

8.9 Exercises 86

9 The MySQL Database Server **87**

9.1 Objectives 87

9.2 References 87

9.3 Overview 88

9.4 Install MySQL 88

9.5 Test 89

9.6 MySQL-Specific Commands 90

9.7 Basic SQL Commands 92

9.8 Create a Database of News Items 95

9.9 Create Ant Build File 98

9.10 Run Targets 100

9.11 Exercises 100

10 Database-Driven Web Applications **103**

10.1 Objectives 103

10.2 References 103

10.3 Overview 103

10.4 JDBC Driver Installation 104

10.5 Setup Libraries 105

10.6 Create a Dynamic News Feed 106

10.7 Test 109

10.8 Exercises 110

11 Database Connection Pooling   **113**

11.1 Objectives 113

11.2 References 113

11.3 Overview 113

11.4 Configure the DataSource 114

11.5 Modify the News Feed Servlet 115

11.6 Create a ServletContextListener to do Initialization 116

11.7 Test 118

11.8 Exercises 118

12 Data Access Objects   **119**

12.1 Objectives 119

12.2 Overview 119

12.3 Create NewsItem Class 121

12.4 Create DataAccessObject 122

12.5 Modify the News Feed Servlet 128

12.6 Test 130

12.7 Exercises 130

13 Item Management   **133**

13.1 Objectives 133

13.2 Overview 134

13.3 Interface Design 136

13.4 Page Design 139

13.5 System Architecture 145

13.6 Home Page 148

13.7 List Page 152

13.8 View Page 157

13.9 Edit Page 161

13.10Create Page 171

13.11Delete Page 176

13.12Exercises 181

14 Web Application Security — 185

14.1 Objectives 185
14.2 Overview 186
14.3 Configuration of HTTPS 187
14.4 The Persistent User Class 192
14.5 Login Functionality 198
14.6 Security Filter 206
14.7 Password Digests 210
14.8 Exercises 216

15 Wiki Application Development — 217

15.1 Objectives 217
15.2 Overview 218
15.3 Project Creation 220
15.4 Persistence Classes 223
15.5 View Page 232
15.6 Edit Page 239
15.7 Publish Page 245
15.8 Unpublish Page 252
15.9 Exercises 257

16 Web Services — 259

16.1 Overview 259
16.2 A Web Service to Publish News Items 263
16.3 Invocation of the Publish Service from the Wiki Application 269
16.4 The Unpublish Service 277
16.5 Security Mechanisms 283
16.6 Exercises 295

17 Conclusion — 297

17.1 Overview 297

Chapter 1

Introduction to Java Web Application Development

1.1 Objectives

- To understand the big picture of web development using Java.

- To learn about web services and how they will be used in this book.

1.2 Overview

The term *web application* refers to a software system that provides a user interface through a web browser. Examples of web applications include blogs, wikis, online shopping, search engines, etc. Web application development became an important discipline following the adoption of the Internet by ordinary users. Many businesses now rely heavily on the web for both internal applications and to provide services to customers, and so there are many employment opportunities open to individuals with web development skills.

Web sites can be roughly classified as static or dynamic. Static web sites are those sites that use a web server to provide access to HTML documents that are stored in the file system. Dynamic web sites are those sites that construct the content of web pages from data that is stored in a database. The databases on which these dynamic sites are built are typically modified as a result of user interaction with site. Thus, users are presented with web pages that are uniquely generated for them based on their previous interactions with the site. The trend is for web pages to be generated from databases rather than being read from the file system.

1.3 Computer Languages Used for Web Application Development

There are numerous languages and frameworks that are used for web application development. Java is one of the older and more established languages in which web applications have been developed. This book covers Java-based web application development using Servlets and JSP. This book also covers the news feed protocol RSS version 2.0, and REST-based web services.

Java is a strict object-oriented language in which all function calls are made to either static methods of classes or to non-static methods that are invoked through class instances. These classes are organized into namespaces called packages, so that unqualified class names do not need to be globally unique.

An application programming interface (API) is a specification that defines how user code can access system functionality. The Java API refers to the specification that defines how Java code may access functionality, such as opening a file in the file system, creating a socket connection with another process, creating a linked-list of objects, etc. For example, the following line creates an instance of the Socket class, which can be used to make TCP connections to other processes.

```
java.net.Socket socket = new java.net.Socket("localhost", 8080);
```

The above line of code can be simplified by importing the Socket class into the local namespace by adding the following line just after the package declaration of a java source code file.

```
import java.net.Socket;
```

The above import statement allows for the following simplified version of the socket creation code give above, in which the package prefix qualifiers are dropped from the Socket class.

```
Socket socket = new Socket("localhost", 8080);
```

12

1.4 The Servlet API

The Socket class is an example of a class that is part of the core Java API, which is available in all standard Java virtual machine (JVM) environments. However, web applications typically additional functionality that is not part of the core Java API. In particular, conventional web applications need to be able to access functionality provided through the Servlet API. Implementations of the Servlet API are provided by third parties, such as Apache, IBM, Oracle, etc. In fact, the Servlet API is provided by something called a web container (or Servlet container), which is defined within an extensive specification called Java 2 Enterprise Edition (J2EE). A web container is actually a web server that loads and executes Java Servlets to process incoming requests from browsers (or other HTTP clients).

1.5 Java 2 Enterprise Edition (J2EE)

The Java 2 Enterprise Edition is a specification developed by Sun Microsystems with input from other major companies in the industry through a mechanism called the Java Community Process (JCP). J2EE describes a set of services that application developers utilize to solve enterprise computing problems. There are many third party implementations of J2EE, including both expensive proprietary implementations, and free open source implementations. The Apache Software Foundation provides a free open source implementation of J2EE web containers, called Tomcat, which is widely used in the industry for web applications. This book describes the use of Tomcat, and does not discuss other web containers.

Tomcat is not a complete implementation of the J2EE standard. In particular, it does not provide an Enterprise Java Beans (EJB) container. JBoss is a popular, free, open source implementation of the complete J2EE standard. The JBoss project itself does not provide an implementation of the Web container; instead, it requires that a third party web container be plugged in. However, Tomcat is the default Web container that comes packaged and pre-configured with JBoss. A popular alternative to Tomcat is Resin and a popular non-free alternative to JBoss is IBM's WebSphere.

1.6   Java Server Pages (JSP)

The use of Java Server Pages (JSP) is covered in this book. JSP is a notation that is added to HTML files, so that per-request functionality can be added to otherwise statically-defined HTML.

It is possible to place all program functionality into JSP files. However, this practice is widely frowned against, because it leads to code that is difficult to maintain after a project grows in size. There are several reasons for this. First, JSP files are compiled at runtime by the web container, so that syntax errors are detected at runtime. By placing this code into Servlets, syntax errors are detected at compile time, which allows syntax errors to be caught and fixed at an earlier point in time. Second, JSP files can not make use of inheritance, so that projects solely written in JSP look more like functional programs rather than object-oriented programs, and thus do not make use of the benefits provided by object-oriented design.

One can move away from pure JSP designs in two degrees: the java beans approach, and the servlet approach. The Java beans approach moves database access and other logic into Java beans, which are then invoked from the JSP. The Servlet approach also moves database access and other logic into Java beans, but also moves controller logic into Java Servlets, and invokes most of the Java bean functionality from the servlets. This book illustrates the Servlet approach.

1.7   Rich Site Summary (RSS)

Rich Site Summary (RSS) is an XML-based format for syndicating content. In this book, we show how RSS can be added to a Java-based Web application from both the client side and from the server side. Rather than develop all the needed code from scratch, we utilize functionality provided by two different open source projects: JDOM and Informa. JDOM is a library that simplifies the processing of XML documents, and Informa is a library that simplifies the parsing of RSS documents. These libraries come in the form of jar files, which are zip files containing the byte code that comprise Java class and interface definitions. To access the functionality provided by these libraries, the jar files must be placed in what is called the classpath. The classpath is basically a list of folders and jar files that the Java classloader searches to find definitions of Java classes. When the jar file of a library is present in the classpath, then its API becomes visible to application code.

There is a tool, called javadoc, that is used to generated API documentation from code and the comments embedded within it. This generated documentation is in the form of HTML pages, and is thus viewed within a browser. It is important to become familiar with javadoc-generated API documentation, because it is the standard means to document Java APIs.

1.8   Representational State Transfer (REST)

Representational State Transfer (REST) is formally an architectural style for building distributed software applications, that is, software systems that run on separate computers and that communicate with each other over a network. However, the term is informally used to represent an approach to building Web services in which message data is placed in XML documents and transported using HTTP. In this second meaning, REST is an alternative to the more complex form of Web services based on SOAP and WSDL.

1.9   Web Services

Software systems that provide programmatic interfaces to other systems (as opposed to browsers operated by human users) are similar to web applications in the sense that they rely on the Internet and usually rely on the HTTP protocol. These applications are referred to as web services. This book provides an introduction to REST-based web services.

1.10   Integrated Development Environments

When developing software, programmers tend to rely on integrated development environments (IDEs). An IDE provides important time-saving functionality, such as syntax checking, code assist and re-factoring. With syntax checking, the IDE will alert you if you have typed a command incorrectly. The term code assist refers to the ability of the IDE to suggest completions to a piece of code that you are working on. For example, if a locally scoped variable is named maximumLikelihoodEstimator and you wish to use this variable in an expression that you are typing, then you can invoke the code assist function to obtain a list of identifiers to choose from. As you type in characters, the list is narrowed to match only those identifiers that match with the characters you have so far entered. Re-factoring functionality allows you to change the name of an identifier in one part of the code, and have the IDE change the name as it occurs throughout the entire code base. These and other time saving functions make IDEs highly useful tools for developers.

1.11 Ant

Ant is the Java version of the make utility that is commonly used to build programs written in C or C++. Without an IDE such as Eclipse, a Java programmer would normally write ant build scripts to perform repetitive tasks, such as compiling and packaging compiled code into archives (jar files). With an IDE such as Eclipse, programmers can invoke commonly used operations such as building through the GUI of the IDE. However, there will always be a need to develop scripts in non-trivial projects to automate repetitive tasks. For this reason, this book covers the use of ant for running database regeneration scripts and for generating various objects needed for application security.

Ant is built into Eclipse, so the user can run ant build scripts through the Eclipse menu system. Ant build scripts are in the form of XML files. The default name of a build file is build.xml. The build file contains one or more targets, each of which perform some job. Each target is comprised of any number of tasks, which comprise the atomic actions that a user can specify.

Ant is a free, open source project maintained by the Apache Software Foundation. The ant build system is well documented, and there are numerous tutorials and articles on its use. This book employs ant in a simple way, so that students can become familiar with its use and the syntax of an ant build file.

1.12 Web Application Architecture

There are many different ways to design Java-based web applications. This book presents a particular design. In this book, we show how to implement a web application that follows what is popularly called the model-view-controller (MVC) architecture. The MVC approach attempts to separate code into three areas of concern: persistence and business logic (model), user interface generation (view), and user input (controller). In java applications, MVC is usually implemented by generating HTML from Java Server Page (JSP) scripts, handling incoming requests with servlets. Persistence of data is done through data access objects (DAOs) or Enterprise Java Beans (EJBs), and business logic is placed inside servlets, EJBs or other classes. In this book, we do not look at EJBs; instead, we use DAOs to provide persistence services, and place business logic within servlets and other classes.

Data access objects (DAOs) are used to provide persistence functionality for objects that can not be stored in main memory indefinitely. For example, the application may have a class called User that is used to represent users of the system. The User object will contain username, password, email and other attributes needed by the application. This information obviously should survive the restart of the system, and so must be preserved in the non-volatile memory such as a hard disk drive. Objects that are instances of such classes as User are termed persistent objects. Although the state of persistent objects can be stored directly in the file system, they are usually stored in a database.

Some databases are object-oriented, which makes storing persistent objects in them straightforward. However, object-oriented databases have not gained wide acceptance; instead, developers use relational databases in which data is stored in tables of rows and columns. The transference of data between objects in memory and tables in the database is not a straightforward process. Consequently, a lot of code needs to be written to implement this functionality. In fact, there are frameworks (such as Hibernate or iBatis) that can be used to simplify the addition of this capability to an application. Use of these frameworks is not covered in this book. Instead, we will develop our own persistence mechanism by placing such code within our data access objects.

There is an alternative to using persistent objects, which is to operate directly on the data within the database without encapsulating it within objects. This approach removes a lot of complexity from the code for small projects, however, larger projects benefit from the use of persistent objects because it simplifies the expression of the application's business logic. This book focuses on an approach to web application design that is based on persistent objects.

1.13 Security

In the Java Web development world, there are several ways to implement security features in an application. This book uses a simple approach to authentication and authorization. A unified process of validating user input is also presented.

1.14   Web Application Servers

Java Web development is usually done using Servlets and JSP. Both Servlets and JSP are standard APIs that were developed through the Java Community Process, which is a mechanism by which the Java language is subject to review and modification by the community. As a result of being developed as standards, there are many competing implementations of what are called Servlet/JSP containers. Some implementations are proprietary and licensed for a fee, such as IBM WebSphere and Oracle Application Server. Others are free, open source, such as Tomcat and Resin. In this book, we use the Tomcat web container. The code that is developed in this book, will generally run unmodified in any Web container. However, certain details related to deploying the application in a particular web container are not subject to the standard, and thus vary between implementations.

1.15   Database Servers

A database server is an essential tool to Web developers, no matter which language, framework or operating system they use. Typically, web developers use relational database servers, although alternatives exist, such as object-oriented database servers. Currently, the most widely used database server in industry is probably Oracle. However, there are some good quality alternatives to Oracle, such as MySQL and PostgreSQL. In this book, we use the MySQL database server, because it is the most widely used free, open source database server.

1.16   Development versus Deployment Environments

One important concept that students are not usually aware of is the distinction between a development environment and a production environment. The book describes how to set up and use a development environment. Specifically, this book details the steps needed to set up a Windows machine to be used for development of Web applications. However, the book does not cover the set up of an environment in which to run Web applications to be used in a business context.

Although it is possible to use Windows as the operating system in a production environment, the Linux operating system is perhaps a more common platform for production servers. Details of installation and configuration of a production environment for Java web applications is not covered. Also not covered are methods used to distribute load across multiple servers, which is a common necessity in production environments.

Chapter 2

Java Setup

2.1 Objectives

- To install Java in your development environment.

2.2 Overview

All Java code runs inside a Java Virtual machine (JVM). The system that provides the JVM is referred to as the Java Runtime Environment (JRE). A JRE is sufficient to run Java code, but it does not contain software development tools needed by developers. For this reason, we need to install the Java Development Kit (JDK), which contains both a runtime environment and developer tools.

Sun provides the JDK in two forms: a Java 2 Standard Edition (J2SE), and a Java 2 Enterprise Edition (J2EE). The J2EE contains the J2SE within it, but also provides additional libraries, additional tools, and a J2EE Application Server. For the purposes of this book, we only need the J2SE JDK.

2.3 Installation

If Java is not already installed on your system, then you should go to Go to Sun Developer Network and locate the download page for the most recent release of the Java Standard Edition (SE) Software Development Kit; at the time of this writing, this was titled Java SE Development Kit (JDK) 6 Update 11. Download and install this package.

Optionally, you can install the documentation titled Java SE 6 Documentation. Alternatively, you can simply access Sun's online version of the JDK 6 Documentation. The most important part of the documentation is the Java Platform API Specification.

2.4 Exercises

(1) Test Installation

Test your installation by running the java command with the version option. To do this, obtain a command prompt and execute the following.

```
java -version
```

Notes

Later procedures in the book may require creating an environmental variable called JAVA_HOME. Also, modifying the PATH variable may also be needed.

Chapter 3

Eclipse Setup

3.1 Objectives

- To install Eclipse in your development environment.

- Learn how to modify the default behavior of Eclipse by associating new file types with the text editor.

3.2 Overview

Eclipse is a tool for building software projects. Such a tool is also referred to as an integrated development environment, or simply IDE.

Eclipse is similar to Microsoft Visual Studio, except that it is free and open source. IBM started eclipse as a proprietary, closed source project. However, after reaching a fairly advanced state of development, IBM converted eclipse into a free, community-supported open source project. The development of eclipse is now managed by the Eclipse Foundation, which is a non-profit organization.

Eclipse can be easily extended by any programmer. Eclipse comes with extensive documentation on how to do this. This is one of the reasons eclipse has gained in popularity. You can extend eclipse in one of two ways: by adding plug-ins, or by adding collections of plug-ins called features.

Eclipse is written in Java, and is primarily used as a tool to build Java projects. However, eclipse can be used to build projects in any language.

```
-showsplash org.eclipse.platform
--launcher.XXMaxPermSize 256M
-vm "C:\Program Files (x86)\Java\jdk1.6.0_11\bin\javaw.exe"
-vmargs
-Dosgi.requiredJavaVersion=1.5
-Xms40m
-Xmx256m
```

Figure 3.1: An example eclipse.ini file that contains instructions to use a 32-bit JVM.

3.3 Installation

If Eclipse is not already installed on your system, go to the Eclipse website and download and install the Eclipse IDE for Java Developers. There is no installation program for Eclipse. Instead, unpack the compressed archive that you downloaded and unpack into a convenient location. You launch Eclipse by running the Eclipse executable file.

3.4 Issues

Eclipse does not run (or does not run well) with a 64-bit JVM on Windows. If you are running 64-bit Windows, then install 32-bit Java and run Eclipse with it.

If eclipse is still not launching correctly for you, it may be that it is loading a 64-bit version of Java. You can tell eclipse which JVM to use by adding the -vm argument to eclipse.ini and have it point to 32-bit Java. Figure 3.1 is an example eclipse.ini file that corrects this problem.

3.5 Configure File Types

In subsequent activities, you will create files with extensions that eclipse does not by default understand. When you try to create or view these files, Eclipse will ask the operating system to run a program that is registered to handle these files types. What we want to happen is that eclipse opens the file using its text editor. To configure eclipse for this default behavior, perform the following steps and see the following screen shot of the preferences window.

- Select Window ... Preferences.

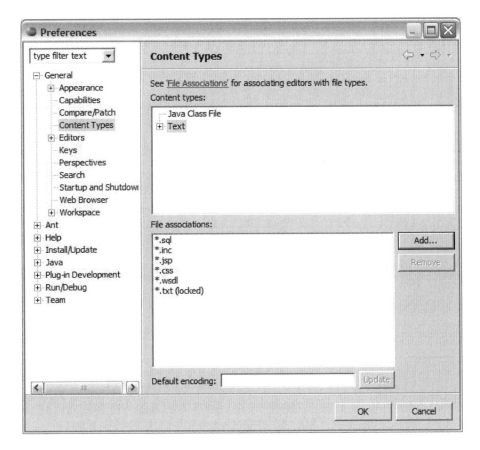

Figure 3.2: Eclipse Preferences Window

- Expand the General branch, and highlight Content Types. (See Figure 3.2.)

- Select the Text node in the tree that appears in the window.

- In the File Associations box, add the following patterns *.sql, *.inc, *.jsp and *.css

3.6 Exercises

(1) Workbench Basic Tutorial

Go through the workbench basic tutorial that is built into the Eclipse help system. This will help you understand how to work in Eclipse. To locate the tutorial, select Help ... Help Contents within the help menu. Expand Workbench User Guide ... Getting Started ... Basic Tutorial.

(2) Java Development Basic Tutorial

Go through the Java development basic tutorial that is built into the Eclipse help system. To locate the tutorial, select Help ... Help Contents. Expand Java Development User Guide ... Getting Started ... Basic Tutorial.

Chapter 4

The Apache Tomcat Web Container

4.1 Objectives

- To install Apache Tomcat in your development environment.

- To understand what the manager application does.

- To learn how to access Tomcat documents.

- To understand and use the tomcat logging system.

- To learn about Tomcat class loading.

- To learn how to perform a deep restart of Tomcat.

- To learn how to manually install an Eclipse plug-in.

4.2 Overview

Tomcat is a J2EE Web Container, which means it is a Web server and a platform to run Java Servlets and JSP. Tomcat is an open source project managed by the Apache Software Foundation.

This chapter guides you through the installation of Tomcat, explains Tomcat class loading issues, and shows how to perform a deep restart of Tomcat.

4.3 Install Tomcat

Go to the Apache Tomcat web site, and navigate to the download page for the most recent release of Apache Tomcat version 6. At the time of this writing, this was 6.0.18. Download a binary release of the Core distribution for your system. Under Windows, you can use the Windows Service Installer or zip file. Under Linux or Mac, you should download the file ending with the .tar.gz extension.

The following command illustrates how to expand a .tar.gz file under Linux.

```
tar -zxvf file-name.tar.gz
```

If you downloaded the Windows service installer, then run it to install Tomcat. Otherwise, follow the instructions in the distribution or on the tomcat web site to install tomcat on your system.

In this book the folder in which tomcat is installed is referred to as ${TOMCAT_HOME}.

4.4 Test

After installation is complete, test that everything is OK. Under Windows run Configure Tomcat, which is found through the Start menu. After starting Tomcat, go to the the following url in a browser to see if tomcat is running.

```
http://localhost:8080/
```

Figure 4.1 shows the resulting Tomcat start page.

4.5 Issues

Tomcat doesn't start under Vista

If you installed Tomcat as a service, you need to run Tomcat as administrator. Right click on the Tomcat Configuration in the start menu and select Run as administrator.

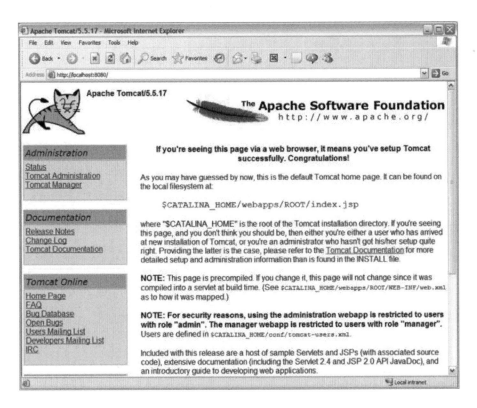

Figure 4.1: Tomcat start page

Tomcat doesn't start under Windows

Open up the tomcat log file *jakarta_service_* * and see if it resembles the following.

```
[2009-01-02 17:08:20] [info] Procrun (2.0.4.0) started
[2009-01-02 17:08:20] [info] Running Service...
[2009-01-02 17:08:20] [info] Starting service...
[2009-01-02 17:08:20] [174  javajni.c] [error] The specified module could not be found.
[2009-01-02 17:08:20] [994  prunsrv.c] [error] Failed creating
java C:\Program Files\Java\jre6\bin\client\jvm.dll
[2009-01-02 17:08:20] [1269 prunsrv.c] [error] ServiceStart returned 1
[2009-01-02 17:08:20] [info] Run service finished.
[2009-01-02 17:08:20] [info] Procrun finished.
```

If this is your case then the problem is that *msvcr71.dll* is not being loaded. The solution is to add the folder that contains this dll to your system path. For example, if the Java binaries are in "C:/Program Files/Java/jre6/bin", then append the following onto your system path.

```
;C:\Program Files\Java\jre6\bin
```

Note that the system path is an environmental variable, which you can modify through Control Panel under Windows. Modify the path in the following example to point to the location of the Java binaries in your system.

You may need to restart your system (or logout and login) in order to make changes to the path variable effective.

If you are using more than one version of Java, then adding Java to the path variable is not advised because other applications may not run correctly. One possible solution is to start tomcat with something like the following.

```
cd C:\Users\User\apache-tomcat-6.0.18\bin
set JRE_HOME=C:\Program Files (x86)\Java\jre6
startup.bat
```

4.6   Configure Firewall

If you are running security software on your computer, such as a firewall program, you need to configure it so that the Tomcat server has sufficient privileges. The privileges needed by Tomcat include the following:

Tomcat should be able to listen on communication ports. (Also called binding to ports.) Tomcat should be able to make connections to other computers on the internet. If you want other computers to be able to connect to Tomcat in order to access your web applications, you will need to open port 8080 to the outside world. However, if your network does not allow for you to accept incoming TCP connections, as is the case in some university wireless networks, others will not be able to connect to your Tomcat server from other computers.

4.7 Manager Application

From the Tomcat start page, follow the Tomcat Manager link. Log in as admin with the password you provided when installing tomcat. This application lets you view the Web applications that are deployed in the server and allows you to modify their state. Figure 4.2 shows the Tomcat Web Application Manager.

Notice there are currently 4 Web applications deployed to the server. In the column labeled Path, you can see the Context Path for each application. For service requests (from Web browsers, or other clients) to reach a particular Web application, the client must include the context path within the URL it uses to reach the server. Web service URLs are comprised of four pieces of information: the protocol (which is http), the fully qualified DNS hostname (which is localhost for the local machine), the port number on which the web service is listening (which is 8080 in the default configuration of Tomcat), and a pathname to a particular service (which is /manager/* for various services available through the manager application). For example, to reach the home page of the manager application currently running in your machine, you would use the URL **http://localhost:8080/manager**.

In this book, you will use the manager application to deploy, start, stop, and reload web applications.

4.8 Tomcat Documentation

Another important link to browse is the link to the Tomcat documentation. Go to the Tomcat start page **http://localhost:8080/**, and follow the link to Tomcat Documentation. These pages contain important information about how to configure Tomcat and deploy Web applications. Figure 4.3 shows the Tomcat Documentation Index page.

Under the Reference section, follow the link to the Servlet API Javadocs. These

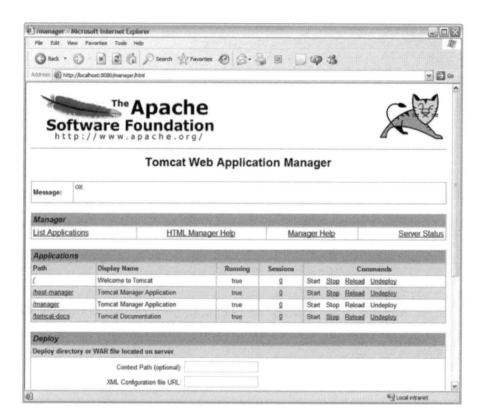

Figure 4.2: Tomcat Web Application

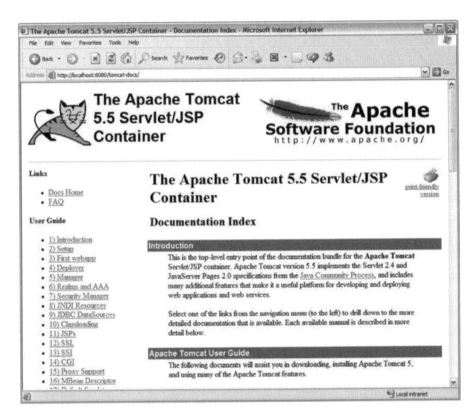

Figure 4.3: Tomcat Documentation Index Page

javadocs (API documentation generated from the source code using the javadoc tool) describe the API of the programming environment in which you will be working.

4.9 Log Files

Overview

When debugging Java Web applications, it is essential that you access the log files. Take a look at the contents of the logs directory within the Tomcat folder to see which log files Tomcat has produced so far. Some of these log files are written to directly by Tomcat and other files are written to from logging commands that appear within applications. For instance, the Tomcat server writes logging information into a file that starts with the word *catalina* and the manager application writes logging information into a file with a name that starts with the word manager. After initialization, Tomcat also writes logging messages for various events, such as when it deploys a new application or changes the state of an existing application.

All of the above log files may contain error messages. It is very important to resolve all errors that appear in these files.

For debugging purposes, it is useful to monitor the contents of these files dynamically. If you are working under linux or MacOS X, you can use the tail command to view changes made to a file. The following is an example running tail to monitor the state of a log file.

```
tail -f ${TOMCAT_HOME}/logs/catalina.out
```

Under Windows, there is an Eclipse plug-in called Logwatcher that enables similar functionality. The next section explains how to install and use LogWatcher.

Logwatcher Installation

If you are not in Windows, then you can use the tail command as described above and skip the installation of the LogWatcher plug-in.

Eclipse should not be running for the following procedure to work, so shut it down if it is. Go to Graysky Plugins For Eclipse and locate the most recent release of the logwatcher plugin. Extract the archive and copy the contents of the plugin folder into the dropins folder with your Eclipse installation. The plug-in will be loaded the next time you start (or restart) Eclipse.

LogWatcher Usage

To use logwatcher, you open a logwatcher view inside Eclipse. Do this by selecting Show View under the Window menu and selecting Other ... Log Files ... LogWatcher. To view a log file in LogWatcher, click on the new icon in the LogWatcher window and browse to one of the Tomcat log files described previously.

4.10   Understanding Tomcat Class Loading

One of the most important things to be aware of when developing Java applications are class loading issues. Java uses a class called ClassLoader to perform the job of loading class definitions into memory, from which the JVM accesses static attributes and methods and creates object instances.

A Web container will utilize several instances of ClassLoader to perform class loading responsibilities. For example, a class loader is instantiated for each web application and used to load classes from jar files in WEB-INF/lib and class files under WEB-INF/classes. Another ClassLoader is used to load classes from jar files found in the lib directory of Tomcat. Other ClassLoaders are also used, but we do not go into any more detail than this.

A ClassLoader locates classes by searching a classpath. For a Java Web application running in Tomcat, the classpath from which class definitions can be loaded include the following directories, where ${project} is the name of the Eclipse project that contains the application and ** indicates recursive descent through all subdirectories.

- Various location under $JAVA_HOME (where Java is installed)

- ${TOMCAT_HOME}/lib/*.jar

- ${project}/web/WEB-INF/classes/**.class

- ${project}/web/WEB-INF/lib/*.jar

The classes under the lib directory are shared by Tomcat and by all deployed web applications. The classes under ${project}/web/WEB-INF are only accessible by the Web application corresponding to ${project}.

4.11   Deep Restart of Tomcat

Overview

Sometimes it is necessary to perform a deep restart of Tomcat, which means to delete all of Tomcat's generated files, which are stored in the work directory. These files include JSP translated into source code and their corresponding class files. These files also include other derived objects related to the configuration of tag libraries and other features.

Difficult-to-find bugs will occur when the generated files in the work directory are not synchronized with the files comprising the installed web application. If you suspect that this condition may be causing problems at some point, you can force Tomcat to regenerate all files in the work directory, which is a procedure that we refer to as a deep restart of Tomcat.

Deep Restart Procedure

1. Stop Tomcat.

2. In the Eclipse log file watch window, close all log files.

3. Delete the files within the directory ${TOMCAT_HOME}\logs.

4. Delete the directory ${TOMCAT_HOME}\work.

5. Start Tomcat.

4.12   Exercises

(1) Servlet API

Locate and study the documentation for the HttpServlet class.

(2) Firewall Experiments

In your firewall system, close port 8080 to accepting connections from the outside world. On a separate computer, try to access tomcat (using the IP address of the tomcat server for URL), and verify that the connection fails. Then, open port 8080, and verify that you can connect to tomcat.

Note: if you are using a laptop on a university campus wireless network, the university may block connections between laptops. In this case, you will not be able to access tomcat running on another student's laptop.

(3) Log Files

Use LogWatcher or other log file viewer to observe how Tomcat writes to the catalina.out log file. While the log viewer window is open and the catalina log file is selected, start and stop Tomcat several times.

(4) Deep Restart

Perform a deep restart of tomcat.

Chapter 5

Java Servlets

5.1 Objectives

- Learn the organization of files for Java web applications.

- Learn how to create a Java project in Eclipse to develop a Web application.

- Learn how to write and run servlets.

- Learn how to deploy a web application in Tomcat.

- Learn how to attach source code for libraries.

- Learn how to turn off compiler warnings.

- Learn how to use the Organize Imports feature of Eclipse to resolve class names conveniently.

5.2 Overview

This section guides you through the creation of a Java servlet. The instructions in this section show you how to write the servlet in Eclipse and deploy it to the Tomcat web server. Actually, Tomcat is also called a *web container*, or *servlet container*, because servlets are placed inside a running instance of Tomcat.

The servlet that we create in this section simply generates a Web page that says *Hello, World!* This simple exercise will help you understand the basic structure of servlets, how to develop them in Eclipse, and how to deploy them in Tomcat.

If you have trouble using Eclipse commands in this chapter, you may want to go through the following two tutorials that are built into Eclipse and accessible through the Eclipse help menu.

- Workbench Basic Tutorial

- Java Development Basic Tutorial

5.3 Project Creation

We will develop the servlet inside an Eclipse project called website. The following steps show how to create a new Eclipse project that can be used to develop servlets. In these steps, we set the name of the project to website. We also associate jar files to the project that contain class definitions that implement the servlet API, which we need in order to develop servlets. These jar files are a part of the Tomcat package; they provide the interface needed for application code to be called by the servlet container.

Complete the following steps to create the website project in Eclipse.

1. Make sure you are in the Java Perspective.

2. Select *File ... New ... Project*.

3. Select *Java Project* and click the *Next* button.

4. Set the *Project* name to **website**.

5. Under *Project Layout*, make sure that the box next to *Create separate source and output folders* is checked.

6. Click the *Next* button.

7. Select the *Source* tab.

8. Set the *Default output folder* to **website/web/WEB-INF/classes**. See Figure 5.1.

9. Select the *Libraries* tab.

10. Click the *Add External JARs* button.

40

11. Navigate to *$TOMCAT_HOME/lib*.

12. Select *servlet-api.jar* and click the *Open* button.

13. Click the *Add External JARs* button.

14. Select jsp-api.jar, and click the *Open* button. (Adding jsp-api.jar is optional at this point, but will be used later when developing custom JSP tags.) See Figure 5.2.

15. Click the *Finish* button to create the *website* project.

5.4 Attaching Source Code to Jar Files

When we use Eclipse to generate code for us, it will obtain information from a class definition in a jar file. When it creates function signatures (function names, their return values and parameters), it uses the identifiers arg1, arg2 and arg3 for names of parameters in positions 1, 2 and 3 of the function parameter list. However, these names are not very descriptive of their function. To make the parameter names more meaningful, we attach the source code for the jar file so that Eclipse will use the parameter name as it appears in the source code. The other benefit from attaching source code is that comments in the source code become visible when you hover the mouse class names and method names. Execute the following instructions to attach the source code for the jar file that contains the servlet classes.

1. Go to the Apache Tomcat website and download the source distribution for the version of Tomcat that you installed, but do not expand the zip file.

2. Locate the servlet-api.jar folder in the Package Explorer view of Eclipse.

3. Right click servlet-api.jar and select Properties from the pop-up menu

4. Select *Java Source Attachment* and then the *Source* tab.

5. Select *External File* and navigate to and select the Tomcat source code zip file that you downloaded in the first step.

6. Figure 5.3 shows the result.

7. Click OK to complete the operation.

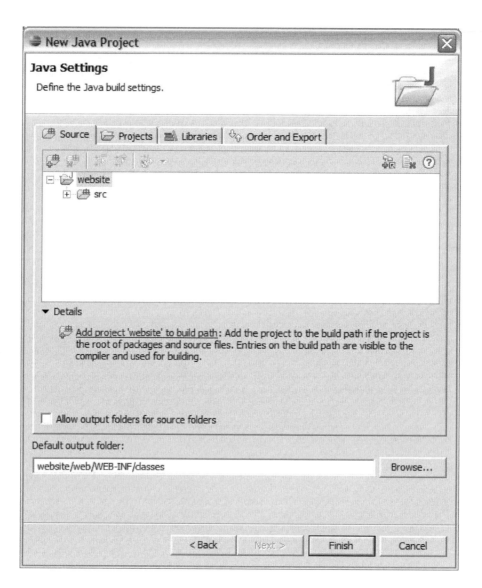

Figure 5.1: Source Tab of Java Settings Window

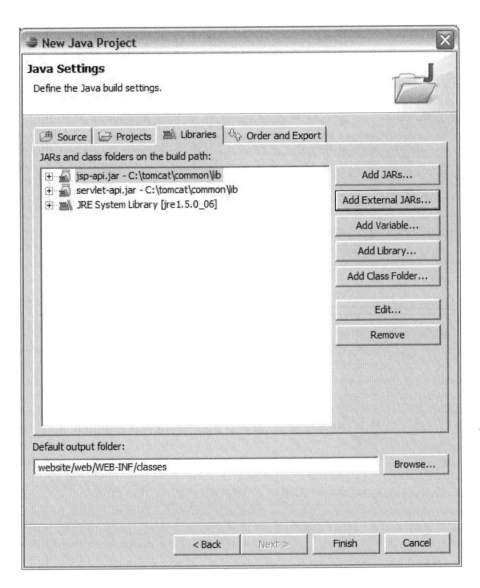

Figure 5.2: Libraries tab of java settings window

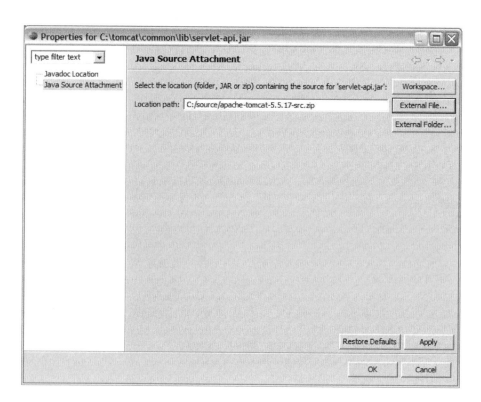

Figure 5.3: Source Attachment Window

5.5   Deployment Descriptor

Inside Eclipse we store files used for the development of the web application within a project folder. The files within the project are used for building the web application and are not necessarily used as a deployable unit of work. We will keep the folders and files that comprise a deployable instance of the web application in a folder called web, which is stored within the project.

Every Java Web application has a deployment descriptor that is located at *WEB-INF/web.xml*, relative to the root of the deployable folder. Because we store all deployable objects under a folder called web, this deployment descriptor will be located at *web/WEB-INF/web.xml*.

The web.xml file configures several aspects of the Web application, the most important information being the servlets and the url-patterns that lead to their invocation. We will initially create a single servlet and have it invoked when the URL requested by the browser matches the url-pattern */home*. To configure this, do the following.

1. Expand the web folder.

2. Right-click on the WEB-INF folder and select New ... File.

3. Specify a name of *web.xml* and click the OK button.

4. In the text editor window that appears for web.xml, insert the contents of Figure 5.4 and save the file.

If you can not edit the web.xml file in the window that Eclipse provides, it is because Eclipse is using the XML editor to provide access to the file. Close this window and right click on web.xml in the Project Explorer view and select Open With ... Text Editor.

Note: make sure there is no leading space in the web.xml file. In other words, the file should start with `<?xml version="1.0"?>` without any space before the left angle bracket.

The url-pattern */home* is relative to the context path that identifies the *website* Web application. Although we haven't specified this yet, the context path will be */website*. This means, for a browser to invoke the home servlet, it must request the following URL.

```
http://localhost:8080/website/home
```

```
<?xml version="1.0"?>
<web-app
    xmlns="http://java.sun.com/xml/ns/j2ee"
    xmlns:xsi="http://www.w3.org/2001/XMLSchema-instance"
    xsi:schemaLocation="http://java.sun.com/xml/ns/j2ee
        http://java.sun.com/xml/ns/j2ee/web-app_2_4.xsd"
    version="2.4">
  <servlet>
    <servlet-name>home</servlet-name>
    <servlet-class>website.web.HomeServlet</servlet-class>
  </servlet>
  <servlet-mapping>
    <servlet-name>home</servlet-name>
    <url-pattern>/home</url-pattern>
  </servlet-mapping>
</web-app>
```

Figure 5.4: Deployment Descriptor web.xml

The deployment descriptor can be used to tell tomcat many things. However, the most basic information provided in a deployment descriptor are the servlets and their associated url patterns. For each servlet in your web application, there should be a servlet element, such as the following.

```
<servlet>
  <servlet-name>home</servlet-name>
  <servlet-class>website.web.HomeServlet</servlet-class>
</servlet>
```

The above servlet element tells the web container to create an instance of website.web.HomeServlet and call that instance by the name *home*. Although it is possible to create additional instances of HomeServlet, normally a single instance is made.

In addition to creating servlet instances, the web container should associate url patterns with these instances, so that when the web container receives an HTTP request from a web browser, it can determine which servlet to use to process the request. The following servlet-mapping element in our deployment descriptor tells tomcat that all incoming requests for *home* should be processed by the servlet instance with name *home*.

46

```
<servlet-mapping>
   <servlet-name>home</servlet-name>
   <url-pattern>/home</url-pattern>
</servlet-mapping>
```

Multiple servlet-mapping elements can be used to associate any number of url patterns with a single servlet instance.

5.6   Create Home Servlet

The above deployment descriptor defines a servlet with name *home* to be an instance of the class *website.web.HomeServlet*. We will implement this servlet to return the string *Hello, World!*. To do this, do the following.

1. Make sure you are in the Java perspective.

2. Expand the website project.

3. Right click on src, and select New - Class.

4. Set the Package to *website.web*.

5. Set the Name to HomeServlet.

6. Make the parent class javax.servlet.http.HttpServlet. You can do this in two ways. The first way is to simply replace java.lang.Object with javax.servlet.http.HttpServlet. The second way is to replace java.lang.Object with HttpServlet, then press Ctrl+space bar to get a list of replacement candidates. See Figure 5.5.

7. Click the *Finish* button.

Notice that there is a warning icon in the HomeServlet file next to the line starting with public class HomeServlet. If you hover over the warning icon with the mouse pointer, Eclipse will display a short description of the warning, which is that you have not declared a field called serialVersionUID. This warning is generated for every class the implements the Serializable interface, but that does not contain a serialVersionUID field. However, for our purposes, creating field serialVersionUID is not necessary. To turn off this warning, do the following.

47

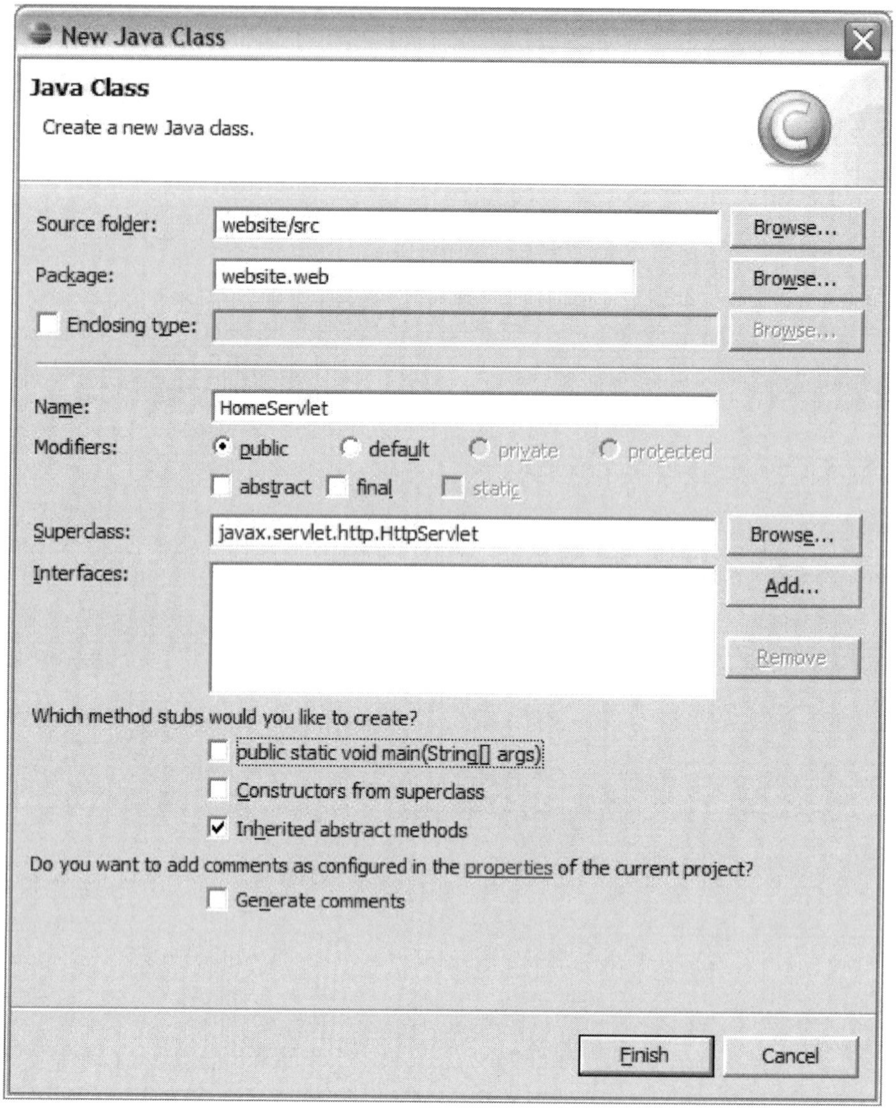

Figure 5.5: Create a home Servlet class

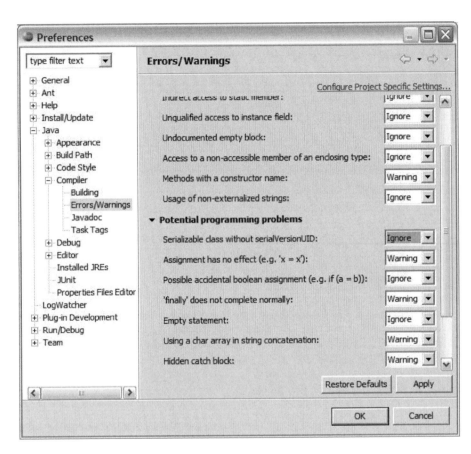

Figure 5.6: Preferences setting window

1. Select *Window ... Preferences.*

2. Select *Java ... Compiler ... Errors/Warnings.*

3. Select *Potential programming problems.*

4. Use the dropdown box to Ignore *Serializable class without serialVersionUID.* Figure 5.6 shows the result of carrying out steps 1 through 4.

5. Click the OK button, and click the Yes button to do a full rebuild.

Now, we override the *doGet()* method we inherit from the parent class. In the *HomeServlet.java file,* do the following.

1. Select *Source ... Override/Implement* methods.

2. Select the *doGet()* method by checking the appropriate checkbox. Figure 5.7 shows the result of carrying out steps 1 through 2.

1. Click the OK button.

2. Replace the body of the *doGet* method with the following code.

```
PrintWriter writer = resp.getWriter();
writer.println("<h1>Hello, World!</h1>");
```

Figure 5.8 shows the result of carrying out the previous step.

When you enter this code, observe the red error icon on the left-hand side of the window. You can read the error message by hovering over the icon with the mouse as shown in figure 5.9.

The error message in this case is that certain classes "cannot be resolved to a type." You can either fully qualify the class names with their package names, as in java.io.PrintWriter, or you can identify the package location of the classes with an import statement. The standard practice is to use import statements.

Adding import statements are easy with Eclipse. To add the imports to Home-Servlet, select Source ... Organize Imports.

Notice the asterisk (*) before the name *HomeServlet.java* in the window's tab. This indicates that changes to the file have not yet been saved. Save the file, and observe the disappearance of the asterisk. Figure 5.10 shows the contents of the *HomeServlet.java* file.

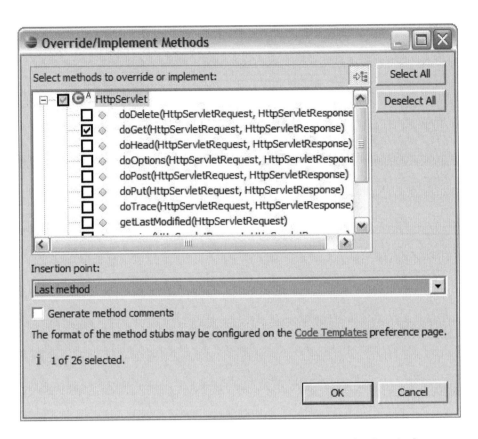

Figure 5.7: Override implement methods window

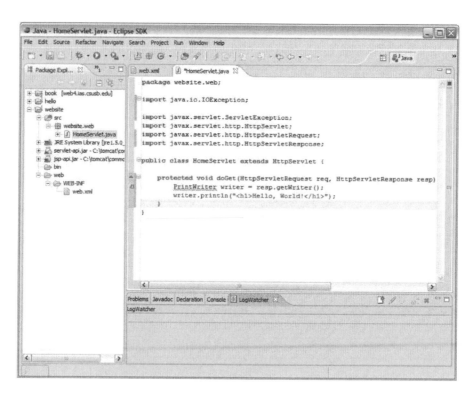

Figure 5.8: Home Servlet javafile

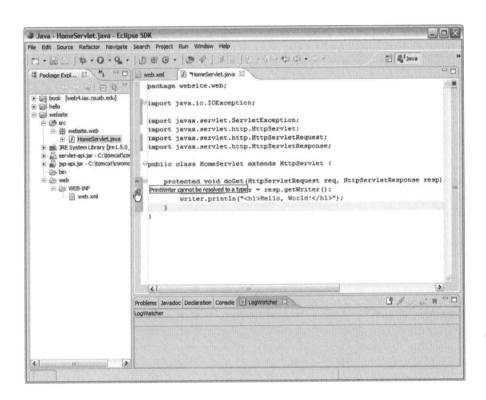

Figure 5.9: Error message

```
package website.web;

import java.io.IOException;
import java.io.PrintWriter;
import javax.servlet.ServletException;
import javax.servlet.http.HttpServlet;
import javax.servlet.http.HttpServletRequest;
import javax.servlet.http.HttpServletResponse;

public class HomeServlet extends HttpServlet {

    protected void doGet(HttpServletRequest req, HttpServletResponse resp)
    throws ServletException, IOException {
        PrintWriter writer = resp.getWriter();
        writer.println("<h1>Hello, World!</h1>");
    }
}
```

Figure 5.10: HomeServlet

5.7 Web Application Deployment

At this point our Web application can be deployed to the Tomcat server. There are several ways to deploy web applications in tomcat, which are detailed in the tomcat documentation. This book recommends that you deploy applications using the manager application that is installed with tomcat. To do this, do the following. (Make sure that you replace ${WORKSPACE} with the actual path to your Eclipse workspace.)

In Eclipse create a new file in the top level of your website project called website.xml with the following contents. (Convert the back slashes to forward slashes if you are working under Linux or MacOS. In all cases, the slash before website in the path attribute needs to be a forward slash.)

```
<Context path="/website" docBase="${WORKSPACE}\website\web" />
```

Go to the manager application and locate the section called Deploy. Set the context path to /website. (Use a forward slash regardless of whether you are working in Windows, Linux or Mac.) Set the XML Configuration file URL to the following, where ${WORKSPACE} is the path to your Eclipse workspace. (Convert the back slashes to forward slashes if you are working under Linux or MacOS.)

```
${WORKSPACE}\website\website.xml
```

Click the Deploy button and then inspect the message section at the top of the manager application web page. If you see the following message, then you need to debug.

```
FAIL - Failed to deploy application at context path /website
```

If the application failed to start, you should check to make sure the path to website.xml is valid. You may also want to open the various tomcat log files and search for an error message that can give you a clue to solve the problem.

If the manager application reports successful deployment, the next step is to verify that the application is working correctly by going to the following url in your browser.

```
http://localhost:8080/website/home
```

If you make changes to Java code in a project, the changes will not be immediately deployed. To see the changes, you should reload the application through the manager application. If you make changes to the deployment descriptor (web.xml) in a project, reloading the application will not work. Instead, you need to stop and then start the application, which you can do in the manager application.

5.8 Exercises

(1) Servlet Mapping Element

Add an additional servlet mapping element to the deployment descriptor that associates the home servlet with the url pattern index.html. Test that the home servlet can be reached in the following 4 different ways.

- http://localhost:8080/website/home

- http://localhost:8080/website/index.html

- http://localhost:8080/website/

- http://localhost:8080/website

(2) Methods doGet and doPost

Become familiar with the doGet and doPost methods by creating web application that accepts a string provided by the user and displays it back to the user. To do this, you need to create an HTML form with an input field and a submit button. In the servlet, you need to call getParameter on the HTTPServletRequest object passed into doPost (assuming the method attribute of the form is "post") in order to get the value that the browser is sending. The key that you pass into getParameter should match the name of the input field you used in the HTML form.

(3) Adding Two Numbers

Modify the web application in exercise 1, so that it accepts two numbers provided by the user and displays the sum of the 2 numbers.

Chapter 6

Web Application Logging

6.1 Objectives

- Learn how to add libraries to a Java web application project.

- Learn how to add log4j logging support to a Java web application.

- Learn how to use the organize imports development tool provided by Eclipse.

6.2 Overview

Software developers usually spend a lot of time debugging code. There are several techniques that you can use to find bugs. One technique is to use a *debugger*, which is a service normally provided by an IDE. With a debugger the developer can step through code one statement at a time as the program executes and inspect that state of variables. For this process to work, the IDE needs to control the execution of the program. When developing a desktop application, you can launch its execution inside Eclipse, set breakpoints, step through the code and inspect the state of variables. However, this procedure is not available to us because Eclipse does not control execution of our code; tomcat controls execution of the code. In order to have these capabilities, we would need to have Eclipse control the execution of Tomcat. One way to do this is to extend Eclipse functionality by installing the Eclipse Web Tools feature. However, we will not cover this option in this book.

Another technique that is useful for debugging is trace statements. In this case, we insert statements at various points in the code to print out useful information.

When this output goes into a file, it is called a log file. One of the benefits of using logging is that logging statements can be left in production code, so that log files are generated in the production environment. This enables the developer to diagnose bugs that surface in the production environment.

Rather than simply using the basic print facilities, a logging framework provides a developer with the ability to set different logging levels, so that logging can be more or less verbose depending on the situation. For example, when the code is running in the production environment, you will most likely record error events rather than the fine details that would be useful to debug a known bug.

There are two main choices of logging frameworks when working in Java: log4j and Java logging API. Log4j is the older of the two and is more widely used than the Java logging API. However, the Java logging API provides the same basic functionality as log4j. We will illustrate the use of the log4j logging framework in this chapter.

In this chapter, you will add logging to the website application you started in the chapter on servlet basics.

6.3 Add the Log4j Library to the Project

We need to add the log4j library to the project build path and the classpath of the deployed application. Go to the Log4j Website and locate and download the most recent release of the log4j library, which is a Java Archive (jar) containing the classes that comprise the log4j library. At the time of this writing, version 1.3 of log4j is a discontinued branch of development, version 1.4 is in beta release, and version 1.2 is in final release. For our purposes, we use version 1.2, because it is the most recent final release. Place the jar file on the classpath of the deployed application by creating the folder *lib* under *web/WEB-INF*, and then copy the jar file into the *lib* folder. If you create the folder and copy the file inside Eclipse, then you are done. This is the approach that will give you the fewest problems. However, if you do either operation outside Eclipse, then you need to synchronize Eclipse with the file system by selecting File ... Refresh.

To place the jar file on the classpath used for building, right click on the log4j jar file in the package explorer view of Eclipse and select Build Path ... Add to Build Path. In the Project Explorer view of Eclipse, the jar file will no longer be visible under the WEB-INF/lib folder; it now appears under the referenced *lib*raries folder. Note that the Project Explorer view presents a logical view of your project rather than a physical view (file system view).

Figure 6.1 shows the result of the above procedure.

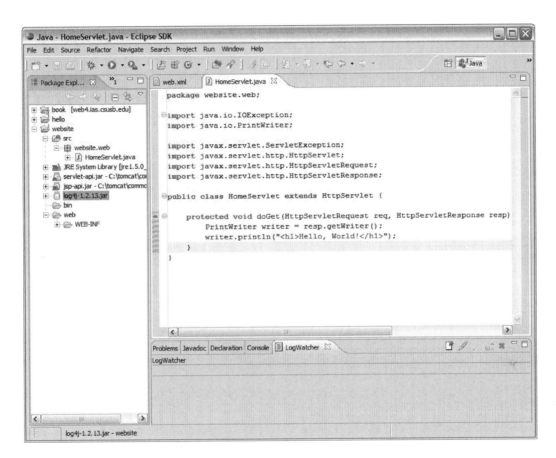

Figure 6.1: Log4j Library Added To Build Path

```
log4j.appender.R=org.apache.log4j.RollingFileAppender
log4j.appender.R.File=${TOMCAT_HOME}/logs/website.log
log4j.appender.R.layout=org.apache.log4j.PatternLayout
log4j.appender.R.layout.ConversionPattern=%d [%t] %-5p %c - %m%n
log4j.appender.R.MaxFileSize=200KB
log4j.appender.R.MaxBackupIndex=1
log4j.rootLogger=WARN, R
log4j.logger.website=DEBUG
```

Figure 6.2: Contents of the Log4j Configuration File

6.4   The Log4j Configuration File

We will configure log4j to write logging messages from our application to a log file that we create in `${TOMCAT_HOME}/logs`. Log4j requires configuration in the application that uses it. The easiest way to do this is to put a configuration file in the classpath. Create the file log4j.properties directly under the src directory and insert the contents of Figure 6.2 into it. *Make sure that you replace ${ TOMCAT_HOME} with the actual path to your tomcat installation.* Note that under Windows, forward slashes work as directory delimiters in the log4j properties file. If you use back slashes as directory delimiters, each back slash should be escaped with an additional back slash.

6.5   The Eclipse Build Process

Because we configured src to be a source directory, Eclipse will copy any files that do not end with *.java* into the default output folder *web/WEB-INF/classes*. However, you cannot see this in the default Java perspective. To see the output folder, you can switch to the resource perspective by selecting Window ... Open Perspective ... Other ... Resource.

Switch back to the Java perspective in a similar manner. Also, there are icons in the upper right hand corner of the screen that can be used to speed up perspective switching.

60

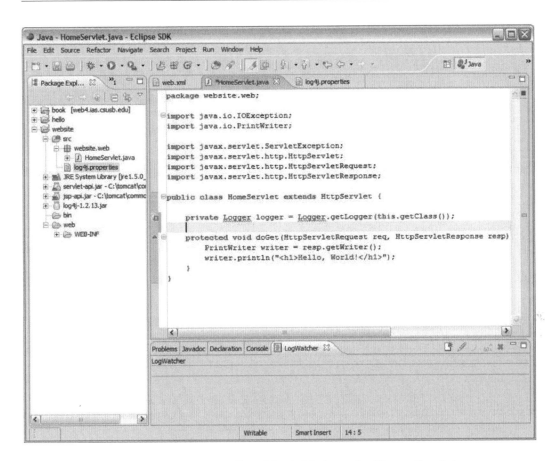

Figure 6.3: Logger Variable Added to the Home Servlet

6.6 Modify HomeServlet

Add the following line of code to HomeServlet to define a private member variable called logger as shown in Figure 6.3.

```
private Logger logger = Logger.getLogger(this.getClass());
```

Notice the error icons indicating that the identifier *Logger* can not be resolved to a type. Hold down the control and shift keys, and then press the O key to organize imports. Because there are two packages in the classpath that contain classes called

61

Figure 6.4: Organize Imports Window

Logger, Eclipse presents them to you as choices as shown in Figure 6.4. The item you should select is org.apache.log4j.Logger.

To study the flow of execution will log a message every time the doGet method of the HomeServlet runs. For this purpose, add the following line of code to the doGet method of HomeServlet. Figure 6.5 the modifed HomeServlet class.

```
logger.debug("Returning website");
```

After making changes to the home servlet, you should reload the website application in the manager application so that Tomcat loads the new definition of the home servlet class.

In order for the website log file to get created, we need to write something into it. Do this by sending a request to HomeServlet by requesting the following link in your browser.

```
\url{http://localhost:8080/website/home}
```

```
package website.web;

import java.io.IOException;
import java.io.PrintWriter;

import javax.servlet.ServletException;
import javax.servlet.http.HttpServlet;
import javax.servlet.http.HttpServletRequest;
import javax.servlet.http.HttpServletResponse;
import org.apache.log4j.Logger;

public class HomeServlet extends HttpServlet {

    private Logger logger = Logger.getLogger(this.getClass());

    protected void doGet(HttpServletRequest req, HttpServletResponse resp)
    throws ServletException, IOException {
        PrintWriter writer=resp.getWriter();
        writer.println("<h1>Hello, World!</h1>");
        logger.debug("Returning website");
    }
}
```

Figure 6.5: HomeServlet with Logging

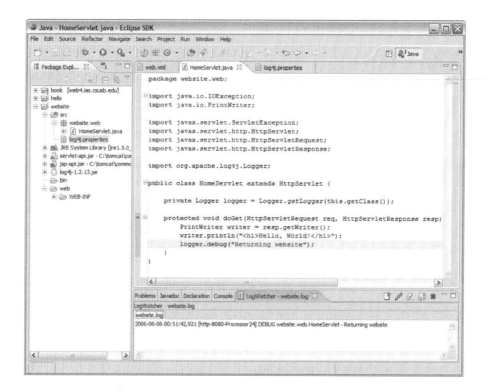

Figure 6.6: Observe The Logging Output In Log Watcher Window

Observe that the file ${TOMCAT_HOME}/logs/website.log} gets created. Open the log file in whatever log file viewer you are using and then reload the webpage in the browser window to see the logging message generated with each reload. Figure 6.6 shows how the logging messages are displayed in the LogWatcher window.

If you don't see the logging statement appear in the watch window, then try reloading the website application in the manager application.

6.7   Exercises

(1) Attach Source Code

Attach the source code for the log4j library. Refer to instructions given earlier for attaching the source code for servlet-api.jar.

Chapter 7

Java Server Pages

7.1 Objectives

- Understand the process by which Java Server Pages (JSP) are translated into serlvets and used in web applications

- Understand how the model-view-controller is implemented in Java Web applications

- Learn how to use Eclipse to override inherited methods

7.2 References

- The J2EE 1.4 Tutorial (See Chapters 12 and 13.)

- JSP 2.0 Syntax Reference

7.3 Overview

Java Server Pages (JSP) is the technology used in Java web applications to mix HTML and Java code similar to the way it is done in PHP and ASP. JSP pages are files that end with a jsp extension and contain a mixture of HTML, blocks of Java code (called scriplets) and other expressions. These JSP files are translated by JSP interpreters into Java source code. The resulting source code is then compiled, resulting in class

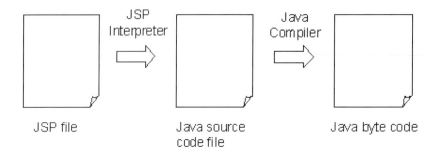

Figure 7.1: Transformation Process From JSP File Into Java Byt Code

files that can be loaded and executed by a Java virtual machine. The process is illustrated in figure 7.1.

The benefit of JSP is that it allows one to easily mix HTML with Java code. For example, consider figure 7.2 servlet. You can accomplish the same result as Figure 7.2 code with the following JSP file.

```
<%@ page import="java.util.Date" %>
<html>
    <body>
        <%
            Date now = new Date();
            out.println(now);
        %>
    </body>
</html>
```

JSP files can be used to process browser requests directly. To see how this is done, create a file called now.jsp in the web folder of the website project with contents equal to the code given above. Then go to **http://localhost:8080/website/now.jsp** and verify that the browser displays the current time and date.

The first time you try to access a JSP file, the web container will translate the file into Java source code, compile the source code, load the new class into JVM memory, and execute the service method of the resulting class. This process takes some time, so there is usually a noticeable delay the first time you access a JSP page. Subsequent requests for the file will be processed more quickly because the container directly

```
package website.web;

import java.io.IOException;
import java.io.PrintWriter;
import javax.servlet.ServletException;
import javax.servlet.http.HttpServlet;
import javax.servlet.http.HttpServletRequest;
import javax.servlet.http.HttpServletResponse;
import java.util.Date;

public class TestServlet extends HttpServlet
{
    protected void doGet(HttpServletRequest req, HttpServletResponse resp)
    throws ServletException, IOException
    {
        Date now = new Date();
        PrintWriter writer = resp.getWriter();
        writer.println("<html><body>");
        writer.println(now.toString());
        writer.println("</body></html>");
    }
}
```

Figure 7.2: TestServlet

67

invokes the service method of the class that was generated and loaded into memory the first time the file was requested.

You can examine the source and byte code files that Tomcat generates from the JSP by looking within the following directory.

```
${TOMCAT_HOME}\work\Catalina\localhost\website\org\apache\jsp
```

Open the file **now_jsp.java** in a text editor such as Notepad. The class now_jsp is declared as follows.

```
public final class now_jsp extends org.apache.jasper.runtime.HttpJspBase ...
```

If you look up the documentation for *org.apache.jasper.runtime.HttpJspBase* you will see that this class is a subclass of HttpServlet. That means our now.jsp file was translated into a servlet. In fact, all JSP files are translated into servlets.

Examine the body of the _jspService method within the now_jsp class. In particular, look at the **out.write** statements in the body of this method. Notice that the content of these lines roughly corresponds to the contents of **now.jsp**. When the translator encounters ordinary HTML content in a JSP file, it generates a write statement to send this content into the output stream directed to the browser. For example, the <body> tag in **now.jsp** is translated into the following Java statement.

```
out.write("    <body>\r\n");
```

The character symbols '\r' and '\n' represent carriage return and line feed, respectively.

When the translator encounters JSP tags (tags with the format <\% ... \%>), it processes the contents of these tags rather than simply writing them into the output stream. Observe that the following two lines of Java code in the sample JSP appear embedded within the translated result.

```
Date now = new Date();
out.println(now);
```

68

```
<jsp:useBean id="message" scope="request" class="java.lang.String" />
<html>
   <head>
      <title>website</title>
   </head>
   <body>
      <h1>Home</h1>
      <p>
         <%=message%>
      </p>
   </body>
</html>
```

Figure 7.3: home.jsp

7.4 Create a JSP

In this section, you will add a Java Server Page (JSP) file to the website application and have **HomeServlet** forward requests to it for generation of HTML content. This design pattern is part of a larger pattern referred to by the term *Model-View-Controller* in which a controller (a servlet in this case) handles incoming requests from browsers, initiates execution of business logic, and then forwards control to a view component (a JSP file in this case) to generate the HTML that is returned to the browser.

Create a JSP file with the following procedure. Create a folder called jsp under **web/WEB-INF**. We will place all JSP in the the jsp folder under WEB-INF. The reason for this is that we want to hide the JSP from direct access by browsers, since all requests (other than those for images, css, etc.) coming from the outside will first pass through one of our servlets.

Within the folder **web/WEB-INF/jsp** create a file called **home.jsp** with the contents from the figure 7.3 program listing.

The first line figure 7.3 JSP file is a useBean element. The useBean element will generate code that attempts to locate an instance of a Java class (called a *bean* in this context) with the name *message* in something called request scope. What this means is that it tries to find a value that is associated with the key "message" in the HttpServletRequest object that the web container created for handling of the current request. Thus, HttpServletRequest is an associative array, which is also called by the terms *map* or *dictionary*. If useBean doesn't find the key "message" in the request

69

object, then it creates an instance of java.lang.String by calling its no-argument constructor. In general, useBean will create an instance of the class specified by its class attribute if the object is not found in the request map.

Next, we modify the HomeServlet so that it creates a String and places it into the request object that gets passed into the home.jsp. In this way, the servlet controls the data that the JSP file presents. This is the general pattern that is followed by MVC-based architectures, which is also referred to by the term *multi-tiered architectures*.

Modify HomeServlet

We need to modify HomeServlet so that it forwards processing of requests to home.jsp. This is done by calling the forward method of a RequestDispatcher that encapsulates the JSP file, which can be thought of as a wrapper around the JSP. We only need to create a single instance of RequestDispatcher and reuse this instance throughout the life time of the application. For this reason, we create this instance of RequestDispatcher in the init method of HomeServlet, since the init method is invoked when the servlet container loads the servlet for the first time, which is generally done when the first request for that servlet arrives.

Add the following member variable declaration to HomeServlet. Remember to *organize imports* to import the javax.servlet.RequestDispatcher class.

```
private RequestDispatcher homeJsp;
```

We will set the value of **homeJsp** in the Servlet's **init()** method. To do this, do the following.

1. Select Source ... Override/Implement Methods.

2. Expand the branch for the class GenericServlet.

3. Check the box next to the init(ServletConfig) method.

4. Set the insertion point to *First Member* (or *First Method*).(This will insert the new method before doGet, which helps to document the workflow through the class in the sense that init is called first and only once.) figure 7.4 shows the result of carrying out steps 1 through 4.

5. Click the OK button.

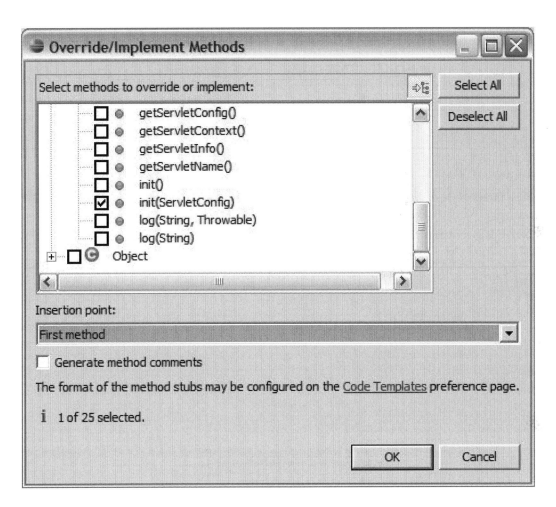

Figure 7.4: Override Implement Methods Window

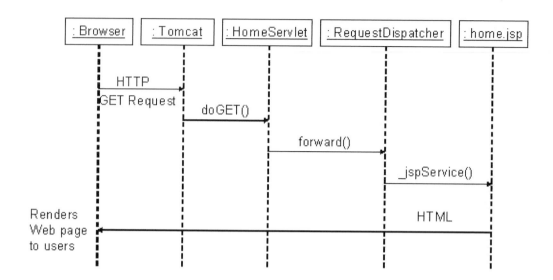

Figure 7.5: Sequence Diagram for Handling

The init method runs the first time the web container loads HomeServlet, therefore it is the logical place to put initialization code. We will use the init method to create a RequestDispatcher that will be used to run home.jsp. To do this, replace the body of the init method with the following (and organize imports).

```
ServletContext context = config.getServletContext();
homeJsp = context.getRequestDispatcher("/WEB-INF/jsp/home.jsp");
```

Change the body of doGet() to the following code.

```
logger.debug("Returning message: bye");
req.setAttribute("message", "bye");
homeJsp.forward(req, resp);
```

figure 7.5 illustrates the flow of execution resulting from a browser request for the home page of the website application.

72

When the user issues the command in his browser to retrieve the home page, the browser establishes a TCP connection with the server and uses this to send an HTTP GET request to the web server. When Tomcat gets the incoming GET request, it parses the HTTP request message and finds that the browser is requesting a resource by the name */website/home*. Tomcat uses the url-pattern elements in the web.xml file to determine how to process these requests. In this case, the requested resource matches with the url-pattern associated with the home servlet. As a result, Tomcat invokes the doGet method of the home servlet. The home servlet sets an attribute (with key *message*) in the request object passed to it by Tomcat, and then forwards execution to homeDispatcher, which passes control to home.jsp. Finally, home.jsp generates the HTML content that is returned to the browser within an HTTP response message. After the browser receives the HTML, it closes the TCP connection with the server.

figure 7.6 shows the modified HomeServlet.java file.

```
package website.web;

import java.io.IOException;

import javax.servlet.RequestDispatcher;
import javax.servlet.ServletConfig;
import javax.servlet.ServletContext;
import javax.servlet.ServletException;
import javax.servlet.http.HttpServlet;
import javax.servlet.http.HttpServletRequest;
import javax.servlet.http.HttpServletResponse;

import org.apache.log4j.Logger;

public class HomeServlet extends HttpServlet {

        private Logger logger = Logger.getLogger(this.getClass());

        private RequestDispatcher homeJsp;

        public void init(ServletConfig config) throws ServletException {
                ServletContext context = config.getServletContext();
                homeJsp = context.getRequestDispatcher("/WEB-INF/jsp/home.jsp");
        }

        protected void doGet(HttpServletRequest req, HttpServletResponse resp)
        throws ServletException, IOException {
```

```
                    logger.debug("Returning message: bye");
                    req.setAttribute("message", "bye");
                    homeJsp.forward(req, resp);
        }
}
```

Figure 7.6: Home Servlet

Notice in the doGet method of HomeServlet that we pass the value of message through the HttpServletRequest object req. As stated earlier, HttpServletRequest acts as a map that associates keys (message in this case) with values (bye in this case). The expression <%message> in the JSP is used to insert the value associated with "message" within the HTML that is sent to the browser. The expression <%message> is approximately equivalent to the following.

```
String message = req.getAttribute("message");
outputStream.write(message);
```

Test

Reload the website application with the **Tomcat manager application**. Then, go to **http://localhost:8080/website/home** to verify that your code is working correctly. Also, check the logging window for the new logging message. Figure 7.7 and figure 7.8 show the web page generated by the JSP and the output of the logging window.

In general, Tomcat will monitor the timestamps on the JSP files in order to detect changes. When a JSP file changes, Tomcat will re-translate the files, so you do not need to explicitly reload an application after making changes to the JSP. For changes to servlet code and other Java code in your project, you need to reload the application through the manager application.

7.5 Exercises

(1) Methods doGet and doPost, Revisited

Rework your solution to exercise 1 in the servlet chapter so that Your solution follows the model-view-controller pattern presented in this chapter.

74

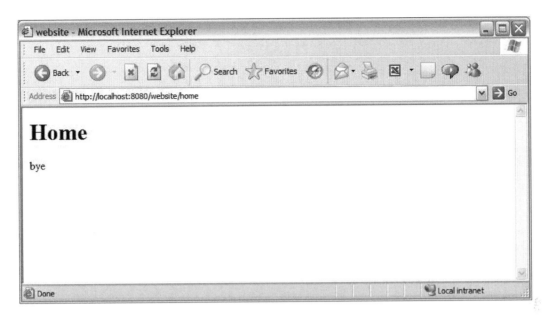

Figure 7.7: Result Page of JSP

(2) Adding Two Numbers, Revisited

Rework your solution to exercise 2 in the servlet chapter so that your solution follows the model-view-controller pattern presented in this chapter.

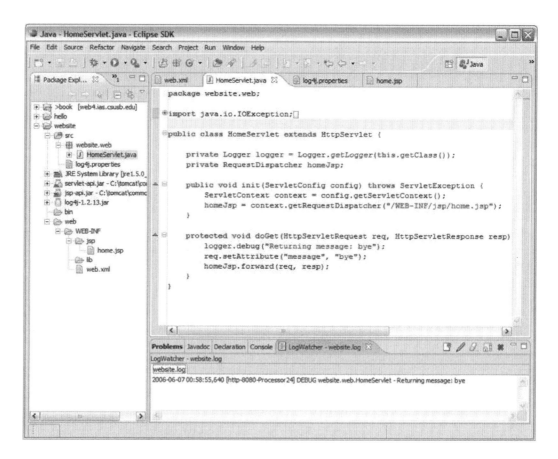

Figure 7.8: Output of Log Watcher Window

Chapter 8

A Simple News Feed Application

8.1 Objectives

- Understand how RSS works

- Learn how to use Eclipse to generate try/catch code

- Learn how to iterate through a list in JSP

- Experiment with the service-oriented approach to building applications by having one application access the web interface of another

8.2 References

- RSS Tutorial

- ROME

- JDOM

8.3 Overview

People interpret the acronym RSS in several ways. For example, you may hear that RSS stands for Rich Site Summary, or Really Simple Syndication, or even RDF Site Summary. Most people simply refer to the technology as RSS. In all cases, RSS is a protocol for providing news summaries in XML format over the Internet.

The following is an examlpe of an XML document that is a news feed. It contains a root element called rss. Under the rss element, there is a single child element called *channel*. The title, description and language elements within the channel element are properties of the entire news feed. Following these elements are a sequence of zero or more item elements. Each item element represents a summary of a news story. In our example, we include for each news story item, the title of the news article, a link to the web page with the complete new article, and a short description of the article.

```
<rss version="2.0">
<channel>
  <title>My News</title>
  <description>This is my news</description>
  <language>en-us</language>
  <item>
    <title>Hello</title>
    <link>http://csusb.edu/</link>
    <description>Hello there.</description>
  </item>
  <item>
    <title>Bye</title>
    <link>http://cse.csusb.edu/</link>
    <description>Come here, go any where.</description>
  </item>
</channel>
</rss>
```

In this chapter, we incorporate a news feed provided by yahoo in the home page of our website application. Diagram 8.1 illustrates the flow of information that will take place.

8.4 Flow of information for RSS

First, the user issues the command to his browser to retrieve the home page of the website application. In response, the browser sends an HTTP GET request to the website application to request the home page. The website application sends an HTTP GET request to the yahoo news feed server to request a current summary of news. The yahoo news feed server returns to the website application an XML document (in RSS format) that contains a list of news items. The website application parses the XML document to extract the news items. It then uses this information to construct the HTML that it returns to the browser.

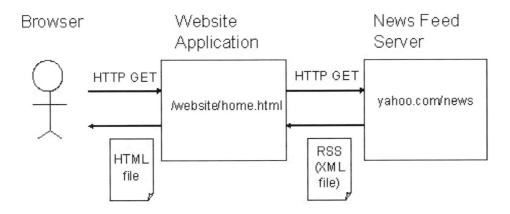

Figure 8.1: Flow Of Information For RSS

8.5   Install Libraries

The code in this chapter depends on ROME, which is a Java API (or library) to parse and create news feeds in the various versions of RSS and Atom. Go to **the ROME project page** and locate and download the most stable version of the library available. At the time of this writing it is ROME version 1.0 release candidate 2. Either download the ROME jar file directly, or download the ROME zip file and extract the jar file from it. Place the ROME jar file in the web/WEB-INF/lib folder of the website project, and add it to the build path. Also download the source code as well. At the time of this writing, this is available as a separate download. Attach the source code to the ROME library using the proceedure described in the Java Servlets chapter.

ROME is not a stand-alone library: it depends on another library called JDOM, which is an API for manipulating XML documents. So, go to the **JDOM website** and download the most recent release of JDOM. The jar file can be found in the build folder inside the archive. Add the JDOM jar file to the lib folder in your project and add it to the build path.

Modify HomeServlet

The next step is to modify HomeServlet, so that it retrieves an RSS news feed and makes the content available to the JSP.

Replace the body of the doGet method with the following.

```
logger.debug("Retrieving yahoo news feed");
URL url = new URL("http://rss.news.yahoo.com/rss/tech");
SyndFeedInput syndFeedInput = new SyndFeedInput();
SyndFeed syndFeed = null;
XmlReader xmlReader = new XmlReader(url);
syndFeed = syndFeedInput.build(xmlReader);
logger.debug("Forwarding to home.jsp");
req.setAttribute("syndFeed", syndFeed);
homeJsp.forward(req, resp);
```

After replacing the body of doGet with the new code you will get icons indicating compilation errors. Most of these errors are due to the fact that the class names being used are not fully qualified (prefixed by their package names) or not imported in the import section at the top of the file. To fix this problem, you should invoke the organize imports operation in the source menu. However, when you do this, eclipse will not be able to determine the package for the InputStream class, because several different packages include an InputStream class. Eclipse will present to you a list of possible fully qualified class names to choose from. The following list shows the choices you should make in this step.

1. com.sun.syndication.io.XmlReader

2. java.net.URL

After organizing imports, there will still be a compilation error. In particular, there will be an error icon identifying a problem with the following line.

```
syndFeed = syndFeedInput.build(xmlReader);
```

If you hover the mouse pointer over the error icon, you will see that there is an unhandled Exception of type FeedException. Use Eclipse to generate exception catching code by doing the following.

80

1. Highlight the entire line that is marked with the error.

2. Select Source ... Surround with ... Try/catch block.

Eclipse generated two catch phrases: one to catch an IllegalArgumentException, and another to catch a FeedException. The code invokes the printStackTrace method of the caught exception. This method will print a stack trace to the standard output stream (System.out). However, in our code, we want to report these and other exceptions in the application log file. To do this, replace the lines that invoke the printStackTrace method with the following.

```
logger.error("", e);
```

Figure 8.2 shows the modified HomeServlet.java file.

Modified HomeServlet.java for RSS News

```
package website.web;

import java.io.IOException;
import java.net.URL;

import javax.servlet.RequestDispatcher;
import javax.servlet.ServletConfig;
import javax.servlet.ServletContext;
import javax.servlet.ServletException;
import javax.servlet.http.HttpServlet;
import javax.servlet.http.HttpServletRequest;
import javax.servlet.http.HttpServletResponse;

import org.apache.log4j.Logger;

import com.sun.syndication.feed.synd.SyndFeed;
import com.sun.syndication.io.FeedException;
import com.sun.syndication.io.SyndFeedInput;
import com.sun.syndication.io.XmlReader;

public class HomeServlet extends HttpServlet {

        private Logger logger = Logger.getLogger(this.getClass());
        private RequestDispatcher homeJsp;
```

81

```java
@Override
public void init(ServletConfig config) throws ServletException {
        ServletContext context = config.getServletContext();
        homeJsp = context.getRequestDispatcher("/WEB-INF/jsp/home.jsp");
}

@Override
protected void doGet(HttpServletRequest req, HttpServletResponse resp)
                throws ServletException, IOException {
        logger.debug("Retrieving yahoo news feed");
        URL url = new URL("http://rss.news.yahoo.com/rss/tech");
        SyndFeedInput syndFeedInput = new SyndFeedInput();
        SyndFeed syndFeed = null;
        XmlReader xmlReader = new XmlReader(url);
        try {
                syndFeed = syndFeedInput.build(xmlReader);
        } catch (IllegalArgumentException e) {
                logger.error("", e);
        } catch (FeedException e) {
                logger.error("", e);
        }
        logger.debug("Forwarding to home.jsp");
        req.setAttribute("syndFeed", syndFeed);
        homeJsp.forward(req, resp);
    }
}
```

Figure 8.2: HomeServlet

Whenever the doGet method of the HomeServlet is invoked, the servlet requests a news feed from yahoo related to technical news. The servlet uses the SyndFeedInput class of the ROME library to parse the RSS document into a SyndFeed object. The SyndFeed interface allows us to conveniently access the information in the news feed using standard Java idioms. The servlet exposes the SyndFeed object to the JSP by placing it in request scope with the setAttribute method of the request object. After doing this, it passes execution to the JSP, which will extract the news data from the SyndFeed object and embed it into the HTML that it returns to the browser.

```
<%@ page import="com.sun.syndication.feed.synd.SyndFeed" %>
<%@ page import="com.sun.syndication.feed.synd.SyndEntry" %>
<%@ page import="java.util.Iterator" %>
<jsp:useBean id="syndFeed" scope="request" type="SyndFeed" />
<html>
    <head>
        <title>website</title>
    </head>
    <body>
        <h1>Home</h1>
        <h2></h2>
        <ul>
            <%
            Iterator it = syndFeed.getEntries().iterator();
            while (it.hasNext())
            {
                SyndEntry entry = (SyndEntry) it.next();
            %>
                <li>
                    <a href="<%=entry.getLink()%>"><%=entry.getTitle()%></a>
                </li>
            <% } %>
        </ul>
    </body>
</html>
```

Figure 8.3: home.jsp for RSS News

8.6 Modify the JSP

Now, we will create the JSP file that constructs the HTML, which is sent to the browser. Replace the contents of home.jsp with the contents of figure 8.3.

Modified home.jsp for RSS News

The code in our JSP file includes references to classes, such as SyndFeed, that need to be either fully-qualified or imported. In our example code, we import these names by using a JSP tag that starts with <\%@ page import...= These lines tell the JSP translator which Java imports it needs to include in the code that it generates. For example, the JSP translator will translate the first line in the previous listing to the following.

83

```
import com.sun.syndication.feed.synd.SyndFeed;
```

You can confirm this by looking in the file home_jsp.java under the following folder.

```
\$\{TOMCAT\_HOME\}/work
```

8.7 Test

Test your application by reloading the website application in the the **manager application** and going to **http://localhost:8080/website/home**.

8.8 Create Publisher Project

At this point, we will begin to develop another web application called *publisher* that will publish news feeds. Initially, this application will simply return an XML document that is stored in the file system. In a subsequent chapter, we will generate this XML document from the database rather than reading it directly from the file system.

For this purpose, create a new project in Eclipse called publisher and set it up in a manner similar to how you set up the website project. In particular, you should specify publisher/web/WEB-INF/classes as the default build folder. You don't need to add any libraries at this point, but we will eventually need to add servlet-api.jar and others in later chapters.

Add the following deployment descriptor to the publisher application. We add the following web.xml file to ensure that Tomcat recognizes our project as a dynamic web application. If we don't do this, some versions of Tomcat will not process JSP files.

Initial web.xml file for the publisher project

```
<?xml version="1.0"?>
<web-app
 xmlns="http://java.sun.com/xml/ns/j2ee"
 xmlns:xsi="http://www.w3.org/2001/XMLSchema-instance"
 xsi:schemaLocation="http://java.sun.com/xml/ns/j2ee
 http://java.sun.com/xml/ns/j2ee/web-app_2_4.xsd"
```

```
<rss version="2.0">
<channel>
  <title>My News</title>
  <description>This is my news</description>
  <language>en-us</language>
  <item>
    <title>Hello</title>
    <link>http://csusb.edu/</link>
    <description>Hello there.</description>
  </item>
  <item>
    <title>Bye</title>
    <link>http://cse.csusb.edu/</link>
    <description>Come here, go any where.</description>
  </item>
</channel>
</rss>
```

Figure 8.4: news rss

```
 version="2.4">
</web-app>
```

Within the web directory, create a new file called news.rss with contents in figure 8.4.

Deploy the publisher application in the same manner that you deployed the website application and verify that you can access news.rss through your browser by going to **http://localhost:8080/publisher/news.rss**.

Finally, modify the url in the website project so that it points to your news feed in the publisher application. Verify that the website application is now displaying your news through the following link: **http://localhost:8080/website/home**. Remember to examine your log files if the application doesn't work as expected.

Note that the website application is communicating with the publisher application by sending XML over HTTP. This inter-application communication is a form of *web services*, and applications built in this way are said to follow a *service-oriented architecture*. text

8.9 Exercises

(1) Include someone else's news

Modify the URL in HomeServlet so that you include another student's news into your home page.

(2) Display More Information

If you go to **http://rss.news.yahoo.com/rss/tech** in your browser, you will see the document that the website application retrieves. (You may want to select the View Source operation of your browser to see the XML document.) Study this document and the ROME API, and figure out how to display more information in the home page of the website application.

Chapter 9

The MySQL Database Server

9.1 Objectives

- Install MySQL for use by web applications discussed in this book

- Understand the role of Standard Query Language (SQL)

- Distinguish between server-specific commands and SQL

- Learn how to design applications that are database independent

9.2 References

- MySQL

- Ant

From the MySQL Manual (version 5.1)

- Chapter 3. Tutorial

- Chapter 10. Data Types

- Chapter 11. Functions and Operators

- Chapter 12. SQL Statement Syntax

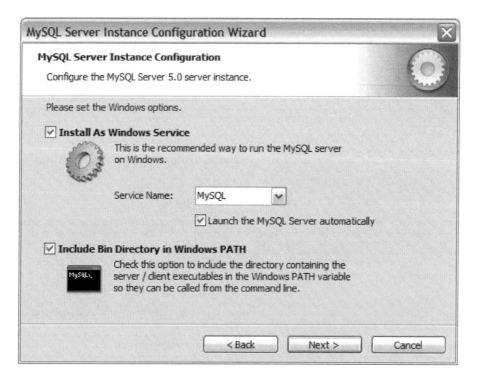

Figure 9.1: Set Windows Options Window

9.3   Overview

This chapter describes the installation and use of the MySQL database server for use in Java Web applications. MySQL is a free, open source database server that has been in development since 1995. Over the years it has matured significantly so that it is now widely known and relied on as a backend service for Web applications.

9.4   Install MySQL

Go to the **MySQL website**, locate the generally available release (stable, production-ready release) of the MySQL community database server for your platform, download and install. Make sure that you add the folder of mysql executibles added to your path. If you are installing on Windows, you can do this by checking *Include Bin Directory in Windows PATH* as shown in the Figure 9.1.

Secure Server Against Outside Access

If you set a weak root password, it may be possible for an attacker to gain access to your system if the Mysql server port 3306 is open to the outside world. To guard against this threat, open the the file my.ini in the MySQL installation folder and and add the following line under the section marked [mysqld].

```
bind-address=127.0.0.1
```

The above setting causes the mysql server to reject TCP connections that are not from the computer with IP address 127.0.0.1, which is the IP address that operating systems assign to the local machine.

Configure Firewall

If you are running security software on your computer, such as a firewall program, you need to configure it so that MySQL server has sufficient privileges. For our purposes, the privileges needed by the MySQL server include the following.

- Mysql server should be able to listen on communication ports.

- Mysql server should be able to query internet DNS.

Although we took this precaution in the previous subsection, it is still a good idea to block incoming connections to port 3306, so that only processes running on the local machine may connect to the server using TCP. If you set this restriction, make sure that the port is still open to local processes.

9.5   Test

After installation is complete, test that everything is OK. In Windows, run the MySQL command line client through the start menu. On Linux, Mac or Windows, you can run the mysql command line client from a command prompt with the command mysql -u root -p. Enter the password that you specified during installation. The mysql prompt appears as shown in the Figure 9.2.

The MySQL command line client is a program that allows the user to submit standard SQL commands to the database server and view the results. It also allows the user to submit non-SQL commands that are uniquely supported by MySQL. In

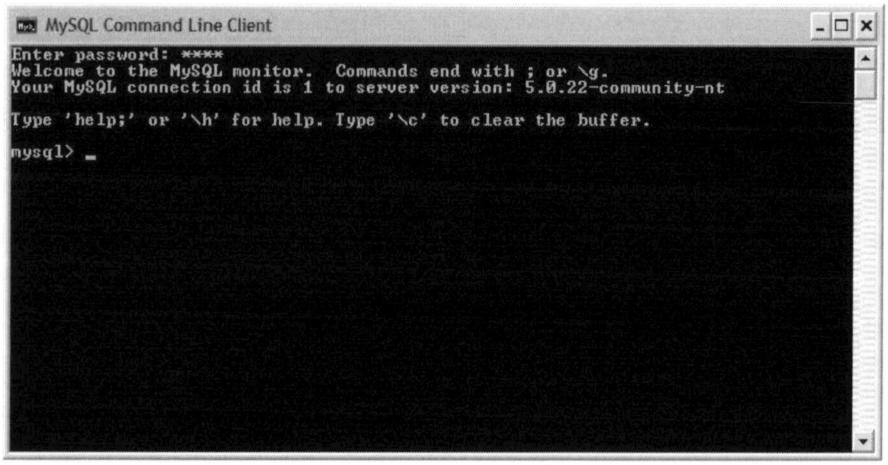

Figure 9.2: MySQL Command Line Client Window

a web application, you will specify these commands as strings in your java code, and submit them to the database through the JDBC database abstraction layer. To test that the server is running, enter the following command at the mysql prompt and press the enter key. Note that the command is terminated with a semicolon, which is a detail that you should remember to perform on all the database commands.

```
mysql> show databases;
```

Figure 9.3 shows the result of the above command.

As you can see, the *show databases* command resulted in a table with a single column. The column heading includes the name Database and the three rows under it show the names of the three databases that were created by the installation program. In general, when a command produces a response, the response will be formatted as a table.

9.6 MySQL-Specific Commands

This section contains description of several important commands that are specific to MySQL that you will need to know in order to develop web applications with MySQL database support.

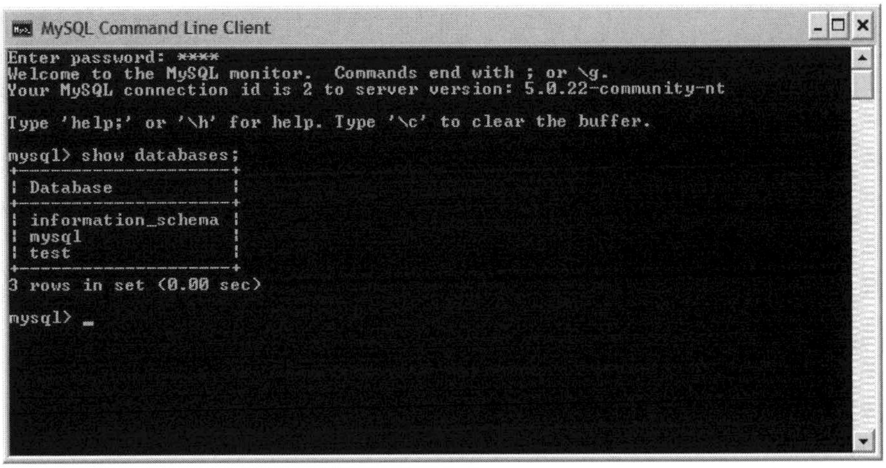

Figure 9.3: Result of MySQL Command

List Databases

The following command lists the databases on the MySQL server host.

```
mysql> show databases;
```

Quit

The following command terminates the mysql command line client.

```
mysql> quit;
```

Cancel Partially Entered Command

If you want to cancel a command that has been partially entered, type , The following illustrates how to cancel a multi-line command.

```
mysql> select *
mysql> from \c
```

Select a Database

```
mysql> use db_name;
```

This command tells MySQL to use the db_name database as the current database for subsequent commands.

Create a Database

The following command creates a database with the given name.

```
mysql> create database db_name;
```

Drop a Database

The following command drops all tables in the database and deletes the database. Be very careful with this command!

```
mysql> drop database db_name;
```

Describe a Table

```
mysql> desc tbl_name;
```

This command provides information about the columns in a table.

9.7 Basic SQL Commands

This section describes several important SQL commands that are part of the SQL language standard, and thus available on most, if not all, relational databases.

Create a Table

```
mysql> create table tbl_name(col_definition1, col_definition2, ...);
```

This command creates a table with the given name and column definitions. A column definition includes a column name, a data type and optional attributes (unique, not null, etc.).

Drop a Table

```
mysql> drop table tbl_name;
```

This command deletes a table. All table data and the table definition are removed, so be careful with this command!

Insert Data

```
mysql> insert into tbl_name values(col_value1, col_ value2, ...);
```

This command inserts a new row into an existing table.

Retrieve Data From a Single Table

```
mysql> select * from tbl_name;
mysql> select * from tbl_name where col_name1 = col_value1;
mysql> select col_name1, col_name2 from tbl_name;
```

These commands show different ways to retrieve data from a single table. The asterisk in the first and second examples indicates that data is to be retrieved from all columns in the table, whereas the third example lists the columns from which data is to be retrieved. The first and third examples retrieve data from every row in the table, whereas the second example retrieves data only from rows in which col_name1 has the specific value col_value1.

In a later chapter, we explain how to use the select command to retrieve data from multiple tables.

Examples

The following examples illustrate the commands described previously. In each example, we show the command that is submitted at the mysql prompt and the result that is displayed to the user. Create a new database called bookstore.

```
mysql> create database bookstore;
Query OK, 1 row affected (0.03 sec)
```

Make the bookstore database the current database on which all subsequent commands will operate.

```
mysql> use bookstore;
Database changed
```

Within the bookstore database, create a table called book with 3 columns. The name of the first column is id and its data type is integer. The name of the second column is title and its data type is variable-length string with a maximum of 40 characters. The name of the third column is price and its data type is double (double precision floating point number).

```
mysql> create table book (id integer, title varchar(40), price double);
Query OK, 0 rows affected (0.13 sec)
```

Insert a new row into the book table. The order of the values correspond to the order of the columns within the create table command, so that the integer 1 is stored into the id column, the string XML Programming is stored into title column and the floating point number 34.0 into the price column.

```
mysql> insert into book values (1, 'XML Programming', 34.0);
Query OK, 1 row affected (0.03 sec)
```

Insert a second row into the book table.

```
mysql> insert into book values (2, 'Algorithms', 42.0);
Query OK, 1 row affected (0.02 sec)
```

94

Display the data in all of the columns in all of the rows of the book table.

```
mysql> select * from book;
+------+-----------------+-------+
| id   | title           | price |
+------+-----------------+-------+
|    1 | XML Programming |    34 |
|    2 | Algorithms      |    42 |
+------+-----------------+-------+
2 rows in set (0.03 sec)
```

Drop the book table. This will delete all the data in the book table and remove its definition from the bookstore database.

```
mysql> drop table book;
Query OK, 0 rows affected (0.08 sec)
```

Drop the bookstore database. This will delete the bookstore database and remove its definition from the database server.

```
mysql> drop database bookstore;
Query OK, 0 rows affected (0.00 sec)
```

9.8 Create a Database of News Items

In this section we will create 3 scripts to manipulate the publisher database. The first script *createdb.sql* contains the SQL commands to create the two tables used by the application: news_item and sequence. The second script *insertdb.sql* contains the SQL commands to insert test data into the news_item table. The third script *cleandb.sql* contains the SQL commands to delete all data from the publisher, including the table definitions.

It is possible to run these scripts from the command line interface of the operating system. However, it is also convenient to run them from within Eclipse. For this purpose, we create an ant build script that lets us run these scripts from within Eclipse. Ant is a widely used command-line based build system for Java projects, so it's useful to become familar with it. We will also use Ant in later chapters to perform

95

other tasks. Ant is built into Eclipse, so there is no need to install anything in order to use it.

Before running these scripts, we need to first create a mysql database called publisher. You should do that now, using the database root account as follows. (Note that the second command is given in multi-line format.)

```
mysql> create database publisher;
mysql> grant all privileges on publisher.* to publisher@localhost identified by
       'publisher';
```

The first command given above creates an empty database called *publisher*. The second command creates a database user called *publisher* with password *publisher* (the argument of "identified by") and with privileges to perform all possible manipulations of the database.

Inside Eclipse, create a folder in the publisher project called *database* and within that folder create a file called createdb.sql with the following contents. (If an external window pops up when you try this, then close this window and right click on *cleandb.sql* and select Open with text editor.)

```
create table news_item
(
   id integer primary key,
   title text not null,
   url text not null
);
create table sequence
(
   next_value integer
);
insert into sequence value (1000);
```

The first command in the above file is the SQL create table command. The command creates a table (in the currently selected database) called *news_item* with 3 fields. The first field is called id and it has datatype integer (an 8 byte signed integer) and it is declared as a primary key. A primary key is a field (or composite of several fields) that contains a unique value that can be used to identify the data in a single row in the table. The database enforces the uniqueness of this field, which means that if you try to insert a new row with a primary key equal to the primary key of an existing row, the insert operation will fail. The publisher application that we will subsequently discuss will follow the convention of making all primary keys integers (8-byte longs in Java) and they will all have the name id in which ever table they appear. The values for the primary keys will have no "business information." Such keys are refered to as *surrogate primary keys or pseudo primary keys* rather than *natural primary keys*, which do contain business information. After examining the publisher application, we will look at an application that implements a wiki. In the wiki application we will use natural primary keys.

Each row in the the news_item table will contain information about a single news item in a news feed. The id field is used to uniquely identify the news_item.

In addition to defining a primary key called id, the first command above also creates a field called *title*, which will contain the titles of news items, and a field called *url*, which will contain the link of the news article to which the news item refers. Both title and url are declared as text, which means they contain character data with a very large size limitation. These fields are also declared as *not null*, which means these fields must contain string data and can not be set to null. Note that setting a not null character field to an empty is allowed because this is different from setting the field to null.

The second command in the above file is also a create table command. In this case, we create a table called *sequence* that will be used to store a single value: the next value to be used for a new primary key. The third command is an SQL insert command that inserts a row into the sequence table. By inserting the number 1000 in this table, we mean for our primary keys to begin from 1000. Every time we use a primary key, we will increment this value.

Note that MySQL includes an *auto_increment* setting for integer primary keys and that many programmers use this as a way to automatically generate unique primary keys. It has the advantage of eliminating the need for a separate sequence table to store the next primary key value. However, this functionality is not part of the SQL standard and is not provided in all databases. For example, PostgreSQL does not provide an auto incrementing feature. For this reason, we use a separate sequence table, which is supported on all relational databases. The benefit is that we can replace the database with any other SQL compliant database without modifying our code. This type of portability is important when a software system may be used by multiple clients who prefer to use a database of their choise rather than the particular database the application is written for.

Create another script called *insertdb.sql* with the following contents.

```
insert into news_item (id, title, url) values (1, 'CNN', 'http://www.cnn.com/');
insert into news_item (id, title, url) values (2, 'FOX News',
'http://www.foxnews.com/');
```

The purpose of insertdb.sql is to insert test data into the database. The above script insert two rows into the news_time table. As you can see from the syntax, the first part of the insert command specifies in a parenthetical list the name and order of the fields (or columns) to be set, and the second part of the command provides in a parenthetical list the values to be placed in those fields.

Create another script called *cleandb.sql* with the following contents.

```
drop table if exists news_item;
drop table if exists sequence;
```

The purpose of the cleandb.sql script is to delete all data in the database including the table definitions.

As we develop the application incrementally, we will need to make frequent changes to the structure of the database. Each time we make a change to the structure of the database, we first run cleandb to delete everything, followed by createdb to create the new structure, followed by insertdb to insert new test data.

9.9   Create Ant Build File

Create a file called *build.xml* in the database folder of the publisher project and insert the contents of figure 9.4 listing into it.

The root element of the build file is the project element. The project element has a required attribute called default, which defines a default target to execute. Under the root element there are various child elements, including target elements. The target elements represent the various jobs that you can execute. Each target element has a required attribute called name, which you can use to identify which targets you wish to run when you run ant.

In our build file, the first child element under the root project element is a property element. Property elements such as this one simply assign a value to a name, which can be de-referenced elsewhere in the build file. In our build file, we assign the value *-u publisher -ppublisher -D publisher* to the name *mysql.params*. The value is a string that contains the command line parameters we need to pass to the mysql command

```
<?xml version="1.0" encoding="UTF-8"?>

<project name="publisher" default="all" basedir=".">
  <property name="mysql.params" value="-u publisher -ppublisher -D publisher" />
  <target name="all" depends="cleandb, createdb, insertdb"></target>

  <target name="cleandb">
     <exec executable="mysql" input="cleandb.sql">
        <arg line="${mysql.params}" />
     </exec>
  </target>

  <target name="createdb">
     <exec executable="mysql" input="createdb.sql">
        <arg line="${mysql.params}" />
     </exec>
  </target>

  <target name="insertdb">
     <exec executable="mysql" input="insertdb.sql">
        <arg line="${mysql.params}" />
     </exec>
  </target>
</project>
```

Figure 9.4: Ant Build File

line client when running the various scripts against the publisher database. Note that there is no space between -*p* and *publisher*.

The first target *all* simply executes all the other targets, which is done by including the names of the other targets in the depends attribute of the all target. The second target cleandb runs the cleandb.sql script. The third target createdb runs the createdb.sql script. The fourth target insertdb runs the insertdb.sql script.

9.10   Run Targets

Run the createdb and insertdb targets by doing the following steps.

1. Right click build.xml and select Run As ... Ant Build.... (Make sure you choose the Ant Build option that ends with the ellipsis ”...”)

2. Uncheck the box next to all [default].

3. Check the createdb checkbox, and then check the insertdb checkbox in that order.

4. Look in the box titled Target Execution Order and verify that the order of execution is createdb, insertdb. Figure 9.5 shows the result of carrying out steps 1 through 4.

5. Select Run.

To check the result of running targets, do the following MySQL commands.

```
mysql> use publisher;
mysql> show tables;
mysql> select * from news_item;
```

Figure 9.6 shows the result of the above commands.

9.11   Exercises

(1) MAX function :

Research the mysql documentation to find out how to obtain the largest value

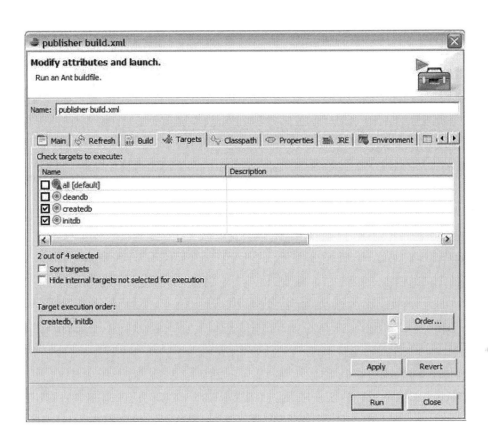

Figure 9.5: Run targets window

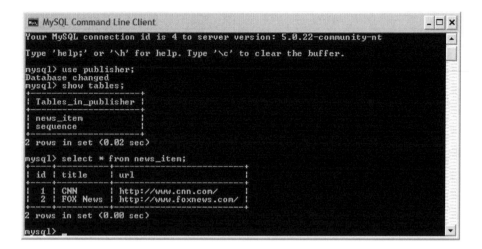

Figure 9.6: Result of MySQL commands

stored within a field in a table. Hint: use the MAX function within a select command.

(2) Table Joins :

Research the MySQL documentation to learn about table joins and then create a database to store information about shirts and their owners. Construct a person table so that it contains information about persons. Construct a shirt tables so that it contains information about shirts that are owned by the persons in the person table. Use surrogate primary keys for both tables and name the primary keys in both tables with the name id. Construct a select statement that generates a table showing the attributes of each shirt including the names of their owners.

102

Chapter 10

Database-Driven Web Applications

10.1 Objectives

- Learn how to access a relational database from within Java programs

- Understand how to generate web pages dynamically from a database

- Understand how to use database connection pooling

10.2 References

- RSS Tutorial

- ROME

- JDOM

10.3 Overview

This chapter introduces the concept and basic technique of generating Web pages from a database. We illustrate this process by converting the publisher application from a static news feed to a dynamic news feed. Actually, what we generate is not exactly a web page; rather, it is an XML document containing news feed data. In later

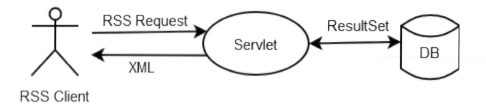

Figure 10.1: Servlet Based System With Direct Access To The Database

chapters, we use the same procedures described here to generate HTML documents, which form the basis of web pages.

Recall that the publisher application returns a static RSS document to client applications. In this chapter we replace the static RSS document with a servlet that dynamically generates the RSS news feed from the publisher database created in the MySQL chapter. We do this by directly submitting an SQL select statement to the database from within the NewsFeedServlet that we create. Figure 10.1 illustrates this architecture. Later, we will use a different architecture: one that isolates database interaction away from the servlets.

10.4   JDBC Driver Installation

Interaction with relational databases in Java is usually done through a standardized API called Java Database Connectivity (JDBC). For this to work database vendors provide implementations of the JDBC API that operate on their databases. From the perspective of the Java code that uses JDBC, there is no difference between databases because the details of communicating with the databases are hidden within the libraries that implement the API.

Because we are using MySQL, you need to visit the **MySQL website** and locate and download the recommended MySQL Connector/J package. Unpack the archive that you download and copy the jar file within it into the lib folder under ${TOMCAT_HOME}.

The reason we place the database driver in the lib folder of Tomcat instead of the usual location in *WEB-INF/lib* is that we will configure Tomcat to create and manage a pool of database connections that all web applications installed with Tomcat will access. For this to work, we need to place the MySQL JDBC driver library in the runtime classpath of Tomcat.

The reason we do not add the MySQL Connector/J jar file to the project's build path is that we do not access any classes or interfaces in this library at build time: only at runtime. Our applictoin only accesses components of the JDBC API that are part of the core Java library. The MySQL Connector/J jar file contains implementations of the service provider's interface of JDBC, which is hidden from our application and needed only at runtime.

Using database connection pools is standard practice because it eliminates costly re-establishment of dropped database connections. Because web applications need to process frequent page requests from multiple clients, the application needs to make frequent connections to the database. Thus, database pooling makes sense in this environment.

10.5 Setup Libraries

In this part of the project, we need to add the jar files for the JDOM, ROME and log4j libraries to the publisher application. For this purpose, create a folder called lib under web/WEB-INF and copy the these jar files from the website project into it. (Note: it's easier to perform the copy operation inside Eclipse. If you do the copy operation outside of Eclipse, you need to refresh the navigator view to see the newly added contents.)

Add these jar files to the project build path so that we can use classes from these libraries in our code.

Configure log4j in a manner similar to what you did in the website project. This involves copying the log4j jar file in the lib folder under WEB-INF and adding a log4j.protperies file in the src folder. Make sure the information in log4j.properties is consistent with the needs of the publisher project. In particular, there should be a line that sets the log level to DEBUG for packages that start with publisher, as illustrated in the following.

```
log4j.logger.publisher=DEBUG
```

The project also needs a reference to external jar file servlet-api.jar. If this is not already in your project build path, then you should add it to the build path. To do this, right click on the project folder and select Properties. Select Java Build Path and then select the Libraries tab. Click on the Add External Libraries button and navigate to ${TOMCAT_HOME}/lib and then select servlet-api.jar.

The reason we do not add servlet-api.jar to the projects lib folder is that servlet-api.jar is already present in the runtime class path by virtue of being in the Tomcat lib folder. So, we only need to add it to the project's build path.

10.6   Create a Dynamic News Feed

In this section, we create a servlet called NewsFeedServlet that generates from the database the XML that comprises a news feed and returns this to connecting clients. We modify the deployment descriptor so that requests for *news.rss* are handled by the news feed servlet rather than having Tomcat return the static document news.rss that we placed in the web folder.

Start by creating a new class called NewsFeedServlet that extends HttpServlet and is located in the package *publisher.web*. See the procedure described for creating the HomeServlet in the Java Servlet chapter.

We are going to write logging messages in this servlet. For this purpose, we declare the following member variable.

```
private Logger logger = Logger.getLogger(this.getClass());
```

The init method of a servlet is invoked by the servlet container prior to using the servlet for the first time. The init method is therefore used to perform initialization for a servlet. In our case, we need to have the mysql JDBC driver register itself with the JDBC system, so that the JDBC system uses its classes to communicate with the mysql database server. In the following, we do this in the init method of the NewsFeedServlet.

In NewsFeedServlet, override the init(ServletConfig) method that it inherits. (The procedure for overriding inherited methods efficiently in Eclipse is described in the chapter on servlets; see the section in which you create a home servlet.) Use the following code for the implementation of init to allow the MySQL JDBC driver to register itself with the JDBC system.

```
public void init(ServletConfig config) throws ServletException {
    logger.debug("init()");
    try {
        Class.forName("com.mysql.jdbc.Driver");
    } catch (ClassNotFoundException e) {
        throw new ServletException(e);
```

```
    }
}
```

The method *Class.forName* in the above code takes the name of a class and returns an instance of Class for it. In our case, this causes the class com.mysql.jdbc.Driver to be loaded, which causes its static initialization code to run. This initialization code registers the class with the JDBC system. Note that the byte code that defines com.mysql.jdbc.Driver is located in the MySQL Connector/J jar file, which we added to the web application's runtime classpath by placing it within *WEB-INF/lib*.

Figure 10.2 shows how to connect to the database, generate a news feed XML document from it, and return the document to the client. Add figure 10.2 code to the news feed servlet. When you organize imports, select the following classes from the alternative presented.

1. java.sql.Statement

2. org.apache.log4j.Logger

3. java.sql.Connection

4. java.util.List

The NewsFeedServlet uses JDBC classes (from packages java.sql and javax.sql) to retrieve the news items from the database. It uses ROME classes (from package com.sun.syndication.feed.synd) to construct the RSS document in memory and it uses the SyndFeedOutput class (from package com.sun.syndication.feed.synd) to write the document into the output stream provided by the response object.

In the doGet method of the news feed servlet, we start by constructing a instance of SyndFeed. This object represents the XML document that we return to clients. We set the feed type, title, link and description for the overall news feed. We then use a while loop to construct the individual entries that comripse the news feed.

Prior to entering the while loop, we issue an SQL select command to retrieve from the database all of the news item data. Recall that a select command results in a table of rows and columns. In Java, this tabular result of a select command is represented as an instance of the ResultSet class. It is returned by the executeQuery method of a Statement object.

The ResultSet contains an internal row pointer, which is initially set to one before the first row. We call the *next* method of the ResultSet to advance the pointer to the

```
protected void doGet(HttpServletRequest req, HttpServletResponse resp)
        throws ServletException, IOException {

    SyndFeed feed = new SyndFeedImpl();
    feed.setFeedType("rss_2.0");
    feed.setTitle("My Local News Feed");
    feed.setLink("http://localhost:8080/publisher/");
    feed.setDescription("This feed was created using ROME.");
    List<SyndEntry> entries = new ArrayList<SyndEntry>();

    try {
        Connection connection = DriverManager.getConnection(
                "jdbc:mysql://localhost/publisher", "publisher",
                "publisher");
        Statement statement = connection.createStatement();
        ResultSet resultSet = statement
                .executeQuery("select * from news_item;");
        while (resultSet.next()) {
            String title = resultSet.getString("title");
            String url = resultSet.getString("url");
            SyndEntry entry = new SyndEntryImpl();
            entry.setTitle(title);
            entry.setLink(url);
            entries.add(entry);
        }
        connection.close();
    } catch (SQLException e) {
        throw new ServletException(e);
    }

    resp.setContentType("text/xml");

    feed.setEntries(entries);
    Writer writer = resp.getWriter();
    SyndFeedOutput output = new SyndFeedOutput();
    try {
        output.output(feed, writer);
    } catch (FeedException e) {
        logger.error("", e);
    }
}
```

Figure 10.2: Code To Connect to the Database

108

next row. If a next row exists, next returns true, otherwise, *next* returns false. Thus, we use the value returned by *next* as the loop condition.

For each row in the ResultSet, we construct a news feed entry, and add this to the SyndFeed object that we created prior to entering the loop. The following shows the XML fragment that we build in this loop.

```
<rss>
   <channel>
      <title></title>
      <item>
         <title></title>
         <link></link>
      </item>
      <item>
            :
            :
   </channel>
</rss>
```

Finally, we use the SyndFeedOutput class from the ROME library and the OutputStream from the HttpServletResponse object to send the RSS document to the client (the website application in our example). Note that we need to specify the content-type of the object we return to the client, which we do by invoking the setContentType method of the response object with the string text/xml. We don't need to specify a content-type when generating html from JSPs because the JSPs will automatically set the content-type to text/html.

Modify the web.xml file, so that requests matching /news.rss are sent to NewsFeedServlet. To do this, insert the contents of figure 10.3 into the web.xml file.

10.7   Test

Restart the publisher application and verify that the news feed servlet of the publisher application is working correctly by going to
http://localhost:8080/publisher/news.rss. You should be able to view the XML document that the servlet generates.
After verifying that the news feed servlet is working correctly, go to
http://localhost:8080/website/home and verify that the home servlet is retrieving your news feed and processes it correctly. The result is shown in the Figure 10.4

```
<?xml version="1.0"?>
<web-app
xmlns="http://java.sun.com/xml/ns/j2ee"
xmlns:xsi="http://www.w3.org/2001/XMLSchema-instance"
xsi:schemaLocation="http://java.sun.com/xml/ns/j2ee
   http://java.sun.com/xml/ns/j2ee/web-app_2_4.xsd"
version="2.4">
   <servlet>
      <servlet-name>news-feed</servlet-name>
      <servlet-class>publisher.web.NewsFeedServlet</servlet-class>
   </servlet>
   <servlet-mapping>
      <servlet-name>news-feed</servlet-name>
      <url-pattern>/news.rss</url-pattern>
   </servlet-mapping>
</web-app>
```

Figure 10.3: web.xml

News feed home page

10.8 Exercises

(1) Add news

Add the following news item to the news_item table in the publisher database and verify that the change appears in the home page of the website application. text insert into news_item (id, title, url) values (3, 'ABC News', **'http://www.abcnews.com/'**); text

(2) PubDate field

Add the publication date (pubDate) field to your database and news feed. Modify both the website application and the publisher application to include this new information. Note that the SyndEntry class contains a pubDate field that you can set.

Additional note: when you invoke getDescription on the entry object in the website application, you should also call getValue to extract a string version of the description

110

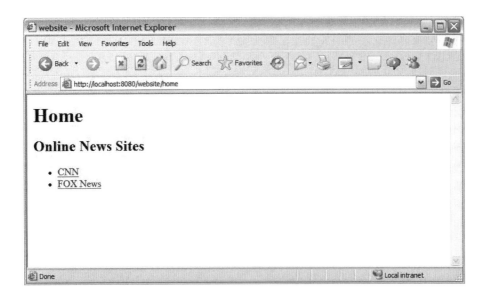

Figure 10.4: News Feed Home Page

object. So, your code will something like the following.

```
entry.getDescription().getvalue()
```

Chapter 11

Database Connection Pooling

11.1 Objectives

- Understand how to configure container-managed data base connection pooling

- Understand the design pattern called *dependency injection*

- Learn how to control initialization of a web application

- Learn about the Java Naming and Directory Interface (JNDI)

11.2 References

- Tomcat home page

- DataSource interface
  http://java.sun.com/javase/6/docs/api/javax/sql/DataSource.html

11.3 Overview

In this chapter, we modify our approach to getting database connection objects. Rather than getting the connection object through the DriverManager class, we get them through an instance of the DataSource class. This is considered a best practice because a DataSource object maintains a pool of persistent database connections in order to eliminate the time consuming step of establishing a database connection each time the application wishes to interact with the database.

```
<Context path="/publisher" docBase="${WORKSPACE}/publisher/web">
  <Resource name="datasource"
            type="javax.sql.DataSource"
            auth="Container"
            maxActive="10"
            maxIdle="3"
            maxWait="10000"
            username="publisher"
            password="publisher"
            driverClassName="com.mysql.jdbc.Driver"
            url="jdbc:mysql://localhost:3306/publisher?autoReconnect=true" />
</Context>
```

Figure 11.1: publisher.xml

11.4 Configure the DataSource

There are two ways to configure a DataSource for use in a Java web application. The first way is to include the library for a DataSource implementation and create the DataSource by interacting with the library. The second way is to tell the web application container (Tomcat in our case) to create the DataSource for us. This second approach is refered to as *container-managed connection pooling* because the web application container that hosts the web application creates and destroys to the data source that implements connection pooling. We use container-manager connection pooling in this book.

We configure Tomcat to create a DataSource and provide it to our application through the JNDI ENC name *datasource*. To do this, replace the contents of $\{WORKSPACE\}$/publisher/publisher.xml with the contents of figure 11.1. (Remember to replace ${WORKSPACE} with the pathname of your Eclipse workspace.)

To make the figure 11.1 change effective, you need to re-deploy the publisher application. To do this, go to the Tomcat Manager application, undeploy the publisher application, and then deploy the publisher application. After doing this, it is a good idea to check the log files to make sure that deployment was successful. If deployment failed, you need to fix the problem before continuing.

11.5 Modify the News Feed Servlet

Since we are using a DataSource to interact with the database, we no longer need the initialization code provided in the NewsFeedServlet. Therefore, delete the init method from NewsFeedServlet.

Add the following static member variable declaration to the news feed servlet.

```
private static DataSource dataSource;
```

Organize imports on the above addition to the news feed servlet and select the following class.

- javax.sql.DataSource

We will follow a pattern called *dependency injection* to set the data source variable. In dependency injection, resources needed by components, such as the data source in our example, are set by initialization code external to the component. The alternative to dependency injection is for the component to acquire its own resources. For this to work in our case, we need to provide a means for external code to set the data source in the news feed servlet. The following code does this.

```
public static void setDataSource(DataSource dataSource)
{
    NewsFeedServlet.dataSource = dataSource;
}
```

We make the data source a static property for 2 reasons. First, to remain general, we want allow multiple instances of servlets to be created in our applications (even though typically only a single instance is created), having multiple data source instances passed into these multiple instances defeats the purpose of pooling. Second, the servlets that depend on the data source may not have been created when our initialization code runs. By using a static property, we eliminate the need of doing additional work to assure that all these servlet instances are first created.

The following code currently appears in our news feed servlet.

```
Connection connection = DriverManager.getConnection(
    "jdbc:mysql://127.0.0.1/publisher",
    "publisher",
    "publisher");
```

The above code should be replaced with the following in order to obtain database connections from the connection pool.

```
Connection connection = dataSource.getConnection();
```

When using database connection pooling, it is important to close connections and their associated objects when finished with them. If this is not done, the pool of available connections inside the DataSource will become exhausted and application threads will block and wait indefinitely for an available connection.

11.6   Create a ServletContextListener to do Initialization

We need to set the DataSource in the DataAccessObject class before the servlets start handling requests. We will do this from a class called Init whose contextInitialized method is called when the publisher web application is loaded by the Web container. For this purpose, create a new class in the *publisher.web* package called *Init* that implements the ServletContextListener class. The complete code for this class is given in Figure 11.2.

```
package publisher.web;

import javax.naming.Context;
import javax.naming.InitialContext;
import javax.servlet.ServletContext;
import javax.servlet.ServletContextEvent;
import javax.servlet.ServletContextListener;
import javax.sql.DataSource;

import org.apache.log4j.Logger;

public class Init implements ServletContextListener {

    private Logger logger = Logger.getLogger(this.getClass());

    public void contextDestroyed(ServletContextEvent sce) {
    }

    private void contextInitialized2(ServletContext servletContext)
    throws Exception {
        InitialContext enc = new InitialContext();
```

```
        Context compContext = (Context) enc.lookup("java:comp/env");
        DataSource dataSource = (DataSource) compContext.lookup("datasource");
        NewsFeedServlet.setDataSource(dataSource);
    }

    public void contextInitialized(ServletContextEvent sce) {
        ServletContext servletContext = sce.getServletContext();
        try {
            contextInitialized2(servletContext);
        }
        catch (Exception e)
        {
            logger.error("Initialization failed.", e);
            throw new RuntimeException(e);
        }
        logger.debug("Initialization succeeded.");
    }
}
```

Figure 11.2: Class Init

We have already configured the web container to create a data source for the
publisher web application. In order to access this data source, we use the Java
Naming and Directory Interface (JNDI) to obtain a reference to the DataSource
object created by the container. In the contextInitialized2 method shown above, the
first thing we do is create an instance of InitialContext. This is the starting point to
locate resources provided through JNDI. In the next line, we narrow the context by
calling the lookup method with the name *java:comp/env*. We named the resulting
context enc because it represents the environment naming context (ENC). We then
perform a lookup through the ENC on the name *datasource* to obtain a reference to
the data source.

In order for Tomcat to call the contextInitialized method of your Init class, we
need to add a listener element to the application's deployment descriptor. Add the
following listener element as a child to the web-app element in the deployment descriptor web.xml.

```
<listener>
    <listener-class>publisher.web.Init</listener-class>
</listener>
```

Later, we will use the Init class to perform other initializations for the web application.

Depending on your version of Tomcat, you may also need to add the following to the deployment descriptor. This is not needed for Tomcat version 6.

```
<resource-ref>
    <description>dataSource</description>
    <res-ref-name>datasource</res-ref-name>
    <res-type>javax.sql.DataSource</res-type>
    <res-auth>Container</res-auth>
</resource-ref>
```

11.7   Test

Make the publisher application reload its deployment descriptor by stoping and starting it through the manager application. Then go to **http://localhost:8080/website/home** to verify that the website application can still obtain the news feed from the publisher application. text

11.8   Exercises

(1) Anticipating problems

Introduce the following errors into the code and describe the effects.

- Omit the listener element from the deployment descriptor.

- Inside Init, replace `compContext.lookup("datasource");` with `compContext.lookup("badsource");`

- Inside Init, fail to set the data source in the news feed servlet.

Introduce an additional error of your choosing and describe the effects.

Chapter 12

Data Access Objects

12.1 Objectives

1. Understand how to abstract interaction with the database though the creation of data access objects

2. Understand the basic operations provided by all data access objects

3. Implement the find and findAll methods of the news item data access object class

4. Learn how and why to create critical sections in multi-threaded Java programs

5. Understand the princple of minimizing visibility and why it is a best practice

6. Learn about the role of an object relational mapping library in a web development project

12.2 Overview

In the previous chapter we showed how to access the database directly from servlet code. This architecture is illustrated in Figure 12.1.

The problem with this approach is that code to interact with the database tends to grow and becomes mixed with logic that directly deals with solving the problem at hand. Also, the code that is used is similar from one instance to the next, giving rise to code duplication. To solve these problems, we improve the architecture by defining

119

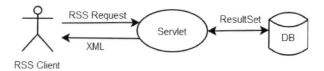

Figure 12.1: Servlet Based System With Direct Access To The Database

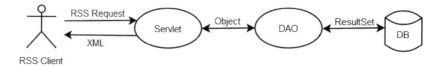

Figure 12.2: Servlet Based System With Object Oriented Approach To Persistence

persistent classes with their corresponding data access objects (DAOs). This allows us to express application logic in terms of manipulation of business objects such as NewsItem and User rather than operating on separate data fields taken from columns in the database. Figure 12.2 illustrates the revised arhitecture.

Normally, code devoted to managing the persistent state of objects comprises a large percentage of the total code. Because this type of code can be generalized, libraries have been developed that provide developers with a framework to implement object persistence in their applications. These frameworks are referred to as object-relational mapping (ORM) frameworks because they provide the means to move data represented as objects in code into, and out of, relational databases. Two well-known open source ORM frameworks include Hibernate and iBatis. Use of an ORM persistence framework is outside the scope of this book. In this book, we look at a simple approach to implementing object persistence. However, as a real application would grow, our simple approach would become more complex, so that adoption of an ORM framework would be more cost-effective in the long run.

In this section, you will define a class called NewsItem that represents individual news items that are stored in the database. The news item class is considered to be persistent because the news item data in the database continues to exist between restarts of the web application. It is also referred to as a business object, or domain object, because it corresponds directly to an entity in the problem space.

You will also define the class NewsItemDAO to provide a means to manage the persistent instances of the news item class. In general, data access object classes (DAOs) hide database-specific activities from the system and present an object-oriented interface to manage persistent data.

When thinking about DAOs, you should remember that each DAO is responsible for managing instances of a single class. For this reason, we append the initials DAO with the name of the class being managed. Thus, the class NewsItemDAO manages instances of class NewsItem.

In our architecture, persistent instances of a class are identified through a member variable called id, which corresponds to a primary key in the database. Therefore, to retrieve a specific instance of a class, you would typically provide the object's id to a find() method of the object's DAO.

Standard methods provided by a DAO include the following, where Object is replaced by whatever class the DAO manages.

```
Object find(Long id);        // returns null if object doesn't exist
List findAll();              // always returns a collection, but may be empty
void update(Object object);  // throws NotFoundException if object doesn't exist
void create(Object object);  // sets the object's id as a side effect
void delete(Object object);  // silently ignores already deleted objects
```

In addition to the above standard methods, additional methods may be needed to support the particular needs of an application. Typically, these will be variations of the find and findAll methods. The following are some examples.

```
User findByUsername(String username);
List findAllExpired();
List findAllExpiredByType(Type type);
```

12.3 Create NewsItem Class

To increase readability, we locate the persistent classes and their data access objects in package *publisher.data*. Create the class NewsItem in the publisher.data package and add the following member variables.

```
private Long id;
private String title;
private String url;
```

Use the following procedure to generate the getter and setter methods for these variables.

1. Selecting Source - Generate Getters and Setters.

2. Click the Select All button.

3. Click the OK button.

12.4 Create DataAccessObject

We will place code that is common to all DAOs in a superclass called DataAccessObject. This will eliminate code duplication that would result otherwise. Create a class called DataAccessObject in package publisher.data with the contents of figure 12.3.

```
package publisher.data;

import java.sql.Connection;
import java.sql.PreparedStatement;
import java.sql.ResultSet;
import java.sql.SQLException;
import java.sql.Statement;

import javax.sql.DataSource;

public class DataAccessObject {

   private static DataSource dataSource;
   private static Object idLock = new Object();

   public static void setDataSource(DataSource dataSource)
   {
      DataAccessObject.dataSource = dataSource;
   }

   protected static Connection getConnection()
   {
      try {
         return dataSource.getConnection();
      } catch (SQLException e) {
         throw new RuntimeException(e);
      }
   }
}
```

```java
protected static void close(Statement statement, Connection connection)
{
    close(null, statement, connection);
}

protected static void close(ResultSet rs, Statement statement,
        Connection connection)
{
    try {
        if (rs != null)
            rs.close();
        if (statement != null)
            statement.close();
        if (connection != null)
            connection.close();
    } catch (SQLException e) {
        throw new RuntimeException(e);
    }
}

protected static Long getUniqueId() {
    ResultSet rs = null;
    PreparedStatement statement = null;
    Connection connection = null;
    try
    {
        connection = getConnection();
        synchronized (idLock)
        {
            statement = connection.prepareStatement("select next_value from sequence");
            rs = statement.executeQuery();
            rs.first();
            long id = rs.getLong(1);
            statement.close();
            statement = connection.prepareStatement("update sequence set next_value = ?");
            statement.setLong(1, id + 1);
            statement.executeUpdate();
            statement.close();
            return new Long(id);
        }
    }
    catch (SQLException e)
    {
        throw new RuntimeException(e);
```

123

```
    }
    finally
    {
        close(rs, statement, connection);
    }
  }
}
```

Figure 12.3: publisher.xml

The data access object class given above contains two member variables: id and idLock. We can place the variable id in this parent class because we will consistently follow the pattern of using an id in every persistent class that we create. Recall that this id is the surrogate primary key used in the database table that stores instances of the persistent class.

The idLock variable is declared as static, which means that a single instance of idLock is available at all times and is shared by all instances of the data access object class and its subclass instances. The idLock variable is used to lock the sequence table in the database so that only a single thread may access the table at one time. If you look inside the getUniqueId method, you can see that idLock is used as an argument to a synchronized statement. The synchronized statement allows only a single thread to enter the code block it contains. Condenting threads are keep waiting and allowed to enter and exit one at a time.

To understand why this is necessary, suppose for a moment that we omit the synchronization and let threads execute statements in getUniqueId without regard to the presence of other threads. Suppose that thread A executes the query to get the value of next_value, which is 1000. However, before it gets to write the next value 1001 into the database thread A goes to sleep and thread B enters getUniqueId. Thread B also reads next_value from the database, which is still 1000. Thread B then updates next_value in the database to 1001. When B sleeps and A wakes up, A will redundently update next_value to 1001 in the database. So far, there is no runtime error, however A and B are in the process of creating separate news item instances with the same id, which they intend to use as primary key values for 2 different rows in the the news item table. The first thread that inserts its data into the database will succeed, but the second thread that attempts an insert will fail because it will violate the *primary key constraint* of uniqueness by using a value for id that already exists in the table. This is a runtime error that will generate an exception.

Our solution for generating unique primary key values will only work in systems that are deployed as single instances. If multple instances of the systems are deployed in order to handle levels of traffic that a single instance can not handle, then the idLock variable will not be shared between instances, which could result in generation of non-unique keys. In this situation, you need to use a different mechanism. This book does not cover these alternatives.

After creating the data access object class, you need to add the following statement to the contextInitialized method of the Init class, so that a data source reference can be passed into the data access object class when the application initializes. Make sure that this statement follows the line that sets the dataSource variable.

```
DataAccessObject.setDataSource(dataSource);
```

You need to organize imports in order to generate an import for the DataAccessObject class. While your at it, you should also remove the following line from Init, since direct access to the data source is being removed from servlets and being kept wholly within the data access objects.

```
NewsFeedServlet.setDataSource(dataSource);
```

Create NewsItemDAO

In this section we create the news item DAO class. For this purpose, create a class called NewsItemDAO in the publisher.data package that extends DataAccessObject.

At this point, we will add functionality that will be used by a revised version of the news feed servlet. Add figure 12.4 implementation of the find method to the news item DAO class.

Organize imports, and select the following class among the alternatives.

- java.sql.PreparedStatement

- java.sql.Connection

The code does not yet compile because the read method is not yet defined. We will define this later.

The find method given above takes a long id as an argument and returns an instance of NewsItem. This method will execute the following SQL select command

```
public NewsItem find(Long id) {
   ResultSet rs = null;
   PreparedStatement statement = null;
   Connection connection = null;
   try {
      connection = getConnection();
      String sql = "select * from news_item where id=?";
      statement = connection.prepareStatement(sql);
      statement.setLong(1, id.longValue());
      rs = statement.executeQuery();
      if (!rs.next()) {
         return null;
      }
      return read(rs);
   }
   catch (SQLException e) {
      throw new RuntimeException(e);
   }
   finally {
      close(rs, statement, connection);
   }
}
```

Figure 12.4: news item DAO class

to locate the row within the news_item table that contains the id passed into the find method.

```
select * from news_item where id=?
```

The question mark in the above SQL statement is replaced by the value of the id passed into find by the following command.

```
statement.setLong(1, id.longValue());
```

The first argument in the setLong method given above is an integer n that refers to the nth question mark in the SQL statement that was used to create the prepared statement (not including question marks that may occur inside data values). (Note that numbering of question marks starts at 1 and not 0.) We pass in the value of the id so that the *where* clause attached to the *select* statement is narrowed to only those rows with id field equal to the one we specify. Because id is a primary key, it contains a unque value, so the table resulting from the select command will have either zero rows or one row.

If the resulting table (returned as a ResultSet) contains zero rows, it means that a news item with id equal to the given id does not exist. In this case, the find method returns null.

If the resulting table contains one row, then the news item with the given id exists. We therefore create an instance of the news item class and set its attributes according to the values found in the returned row. This job is handled by a separate read method. The reason we place the operations into a separate method is that we will need to carry out the same operations for other methods in the news item DAO. By placing these common operations in their own read method, we reduce code duplication. Minimizing code duplication is important because it makes the program easier to manage, since changes to common functionality only need to by made in one place.

The following listing provides the implementation of the read method, which you should add to the news item DAO class.

```
private NewsItem read(ResultSet rs) throws SQLException {
    Long id = new Long(rs.getLong("id"));
    String title = rs.getString("title");
```

```
    String url = rs.getString("url");
    NewsItem newsItem = new NewsItem();
    newsItem.setId(id);
    newsItem.setTitle(title);
    newsItem.setUrl(url);
    return newsItem;
}
```

We declare the read method as private because only methods within the news item DAO will call read. If we give the method greater visibility by declaring it public, the code will still function as needed; however, we would be violating a widely accepted best practice of limiting visibility as much as possible. The benefit of following this practice is that it improves readability of the code. If we make the read method private, the reader of the code knows that only internal methods will call the read method. If we declared it as public, the reader of the code may be misled into thinking that code outside the class is calling into the read method.

The above find method will be used in the next chapter by various servlets to extract a single news item from the database. However, the news feed servlet that we are developing in this chapter needs to extract all news items from the database. For this purpose, add figure 12.5 implementation of the findAll method to the news item DAO. Organize imports, and select the following class among the alternatives.

- java.util.List

The findAll method selects all the rows and columns of the news_item table and then populates a linked list with instances of the news item class and return this to the caller. If no news items a found, we return a linked list that is empty. Notice that for every row in the result set, we call the read method to extract column values and place them in a news item instance.

12.5 Modify the News Feed Servlet

The news feed servlet will no longer access the database directly. For this reason, you can remove from it the member variable dataSource and its corresponding set method. (Also, you need to remove the call to setDataSource in the Init class.)

Replace the try/catch block in the doGet method of the news feed servlet class with the following code that extracts the data through the NewsItem and NewsItem-DAO classes.

```
public List<NewsItem> findAll() {
   LinkedList<NewsItem> newsItems = new LinkedList<NewsItem>();
   ResultSet rs = null;
   PreparedStatement statement = null;
   Connection connection = null;
   try {
      connection = getConnection();
      String sql = "select * from news_item order by id";
      statement = connection.prepareStatement(sql);
      rs = statement.executeQuery();
      while (rs.next()) {
         NewsItem newsItem = read(rs);
         newsItems.add(newsItem);
      }
      return newsItems;
   }
   catch (SQLException e) {
      throw new RuntimeException(e);
   }
   finally {
      close(rs, statement, connection);
   }
}
```

Figure 12.5: findAll method

```
List<NewsItem> newsItems = new NewsItemDAO().findAll();
Iterator<NewsItem> it = newsItems.iterator();
while (it.hasNext()) {
   NewsItem newsItem = (NewsItem) it.next();
   String title = newsItem.getTitle();
   String url = newsItem.getUrl();
   SyndEntry entry = new SyndEntryImpl();
   entry.setTitle(title);
   entry.setLink(url);
   entries.add(entry);
}
```

Organize imports and select the following classes from the alternatives.

- java.util.Iterator

12.6   Test

Reload the publisher application and verify that the application can still obtain the news feed from the publisher application by going to *http://localhost:8080/website/home*.

12.7   Exercises

(1) PubDate field

If you have not carried over the publication date field from your solution to the PubDate exercise in the database-driven web applications chapter, then incorporate it back into the publisher and website web applications.

(2) Description field

Modify the publisher application so that it contains a description field in the news_item table and includes this in the XML returned by the news item servlet.

The ROME library handles the description field a little differently from other fields such as title and link. The following is some example code to get started with. See the ROME API documentation for details.

```
SyndContent syndContent = new SyndContentImpl();
syndContent.setType("text/plain");
syndContent.setValue(description);
entry.setDescription(syndContent);
```

Modify the website application so that it displays a descritpion for each new item.

Chapter 13

Item Management

13.1 Objectives

1. Understand how to implement item management

2. Learn about use case diagrams, page flow diagrams and sequence diagrams

3. Learn how to develop a page layout mechanism in JSP

4. Understand what is meant by a layered architecture

5. Learn how to process form submissions

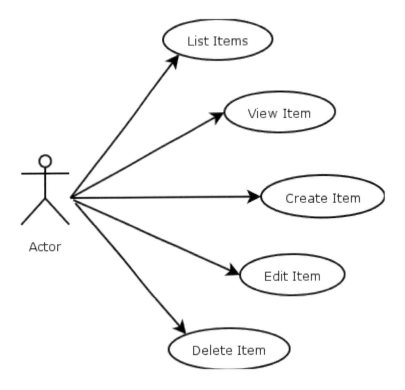

Figure 13.1: UseCase Diagram

13.2 Overview

A common feature that software provides to users is the ability to manage a collection of items. In this chapter, we implement this functionality in the publisher application, so that users can manage the news items that are stored in the publisher database.

Use Cases

Figure 13.1 shows the use case diagram which summarizes the use cases that our added functionality must support.

In a larger application, it is not usually necessary to enumerate the detailed use cases shown in Figure 13.1. Instead, these use cases are compressed into a single use case called something like *manage items* as illustrated in Figure 13.2.

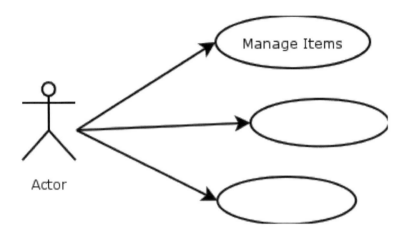

Figure 13.2: Single UseCase For Managing Items

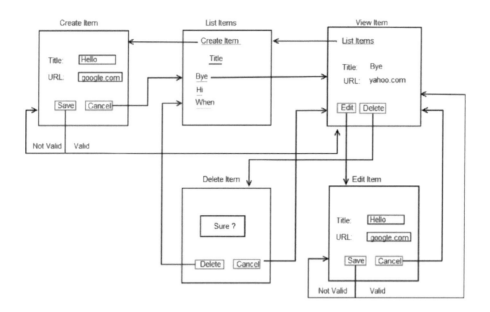

Figure 13.3: Page Flow Diagram

13.3 Interface Design

A page flow diagram describes how the user goes from one page to the next in response to user input. The page flow diagram can be used as a basis for designing the servlets and JSP. Figure 13.3 shows the page flow diagram for the item management functionality that will be added to the publisher applciation in this chapter.

Page Flow Diagram

The page flow diagram above illustrates the connections between a subset of pages in the application. Not shown in the diagram is the publisher application home page. From the home page, the user will be able to go to the list items page or the create item page. These two transitions will be made possible through a global menu (appearing on every page) that provides the following choices.

- List news items

- Create news item

136

• Logout

The logout operation available in the global menu will be dicsussed in a later chapter.

The purpose of the create item page is to allow users to input data for the creation of new items. This page will therefore contain a form with fields empty or set to default values. A user chooses to either save the newly specified item or cancel the creation operation. When a user chooses to save the new item, the data being submitted is subjected to a validation test. A validation test decides if the data being submitted violates any constraints placed on the data. For example, in our application, the title field and the link fields cannot be empty. If a user submits an empty value for either of these fields, the submission will fail the validation test. If the submission fails validation, the user is kept on the item creation page, but the system adds notation to inform the user of the problems. If the data passes validation, the user is presented with the view item page. The purpose of sending the user to the view page is that it allows the user to see that the new item has been created in the system. The alternative to going to the view item page is to go to the list items page, because the user can also see on this page that the new item has been created, becuase it now appears in the list. However, if the list is long, the user must expend mental effort to search the list and locate the new item. However, only a summary of the new item appears in the list items page,\ so that user may suffer some doubt that all the details he or she specified entered into the system correctly. The user would need to go to the view item page in order to verify this.

The list items page lists all the items in the system. This can be developed, of course, so that the user can specify a filter in order to generate smaller lists that contain only items that satisfy the criteria in the filter. For example, the user might be given the choice of listing only news feed entries that fall within a given category of news. From list items page, the user can navigate to an individual news item, which is displayed in the view item page.

The view item page presents the detailed information associated with an individual item. The particular item that is being viewed on the page is considered the current item that is subject to the two available operations of delete and edit.

The delete item page is a confirmation page that is arrived at when the user selects to delete the current item shown in the view item page. It's important to provide a confirm step, because the user may have mistakenly selected the delete operation from the view item page. If the user confirms the delete, the item is deleted from the system and the user is sent to the list items page. The user can see that the item has been deleted because it no longer appears with the list items page. If the user cancels the delete operation, the user is sent back to the view page from where he or she came. Bringing the user back to the view page allows the user to verify that the delete operation was canceled.

It's important to use unambiguous and simple language in all the pages, but especially in the delete page. Consider the following two alternatives for the wording on the delete page.

```
Are you sure you wish to delete this item?   yes    no

Are you sure you wish to delete this item?   delete    cancel
```

The second wording is preferable to the first because the two answers can almost stand independently of the question. From the question, the user understands that the delete operation is being postponed until he or she confirms at this point. The *yes/no* answers require the user to refer back to the question to make sure that the answer given is correct, whereas the *delete/cancel* answers can be understood in relation to the simpler notion that the system is asking the user to confirm the delete operation.

The edit page allows the user to change data associated with the item. This page is the same as the create item page except for two differences. First, the edit item page presents a form with all fields set to the current values of the item, rather than being blank or set to default values. Second, when the user cancels from the edit page, the user is taken back to the view item page rather than the list items page.

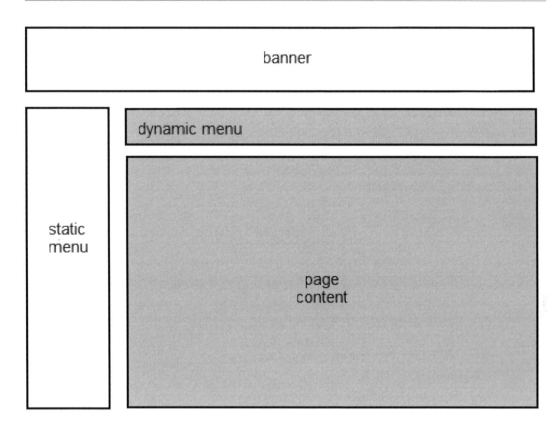

Figure 13.4: Page Layout Of Home Page

13.4 Page Design

Page Layout

We will use a single layout to design all web pages in the application. The layout is shown in Figure 13.4.

The areas that are filled with green are considered dynamic page content. The banner and static menu are generated from top.inc and the footer is generated from bottom.inc.

Page Example

As a next step in the process, we build a sample web page that ressembles what would be produced from a typical interaction with the system. For this purpose, we choose to create an *example of the view item page*. The purpose of the view item page is to show the details of a particular news feed entry. From within this page, the user should be able to start an edit or a delete operation for the currently viewed news item.

The page contains a horizontal banner that should identify the application, which is the publisher application.

Under the horizontal banner, there is a dashed line that separates a left column from a right column. The left column contains a static menu of choices that will be present on every page in the application. We refer to this menu as the *global menu*. The right column contains a page specific menu and page specific content.

Figure 13.5 is the HTML of the example view item page.

```
<html>

<head>
  <title>Publisher Application</title>
</head>

<body style="margin: 0; padding: 0">

<table width="728"
          cellspacing="0"
          cellpadding="0"
          style="padding: 0; margin: 0; border-collapse: collapse">
<tr style="padding: 0; margin: 0">
<td width="728"
      colspan="2"
      style="padding: 0; margin: 0"><img
         src="logo.gif"
         style="padding: 0; margin"></td>
</tr>
<tr style="padding: 0; margin: 0">
<td width="728"
      colspan="2"
      style="padding: 0; margin: 0"><div
        style="padding: 0;
                  margin: 0;
                  text-align: center;
```

```
                        font-size: small;
                        background-color: #99CCCC">
        Publisher Application
</div></td>
</tr>
<tr>
    <td rowspan="2"
          width="240"
          valign="top">
        <div style="height: 500px; padding: 20px; border-right: 3px dashed;
                    margin-right: 20px">
            <a href="list-news-items">List News Items</a><br/>
            <a href="create-news-item">Create News Item</a><br/>
            <a href="logout">Logout</a> <br/>
        </div>
    </td>
    <td width="488">
        <div style="margin-top: 12px; margin-bottom: 12 px">
<!-- start of page-specific menu -->
            <a href="edit?item=3">edit</a>
            <a href="delete?item=3">delete</a>
<!-- end of page-specific menu -->
        </div>
    </td>
  </tr>
  <tr>
    <td valign="top">
<!-- start of page content -->
        <h1 style="font-size: larger">View News Item</h1>
        <p>Title: California State University San Bernardino</p>
        <p>Link: <a href="http://csusb.edu/">http://csusb.edu/</a></p>
<!-- end of page content -->
    </td>
  </tr>
</table>

</body>
</html>
```

Figure 13.5: view item page

There are 4 HTML comments in Figure 13.5 listing that delimit the two areas that will change between web pages. All other areas in the above example can be identical between web pages. If we keep the static content in a single location, it will be much easier to make global changes to the design of our pages. One way to do this is to carve the example HTML into three separate pieces and store them in files to be included by the JSP files that need them. The structure of our JSP files will then be as follows.

```
<%@ include file="top.inc" %>
  <!-- page menu -->
<%@ include file="middle.inc" %>
  <!-- page content -->
<%@ include file="bottom.inc" %>
```

You should create these 3 files now, placing them in web/WEB-INF/jsp. When you are done, the 3 files should look like figure 13.6, figure 13.7 and figure 13.8.

```
<html>

<head>
  <title>Publisher Application</title>
</head>

<body style="margin: 0; padding: 0">

<table width="728"
          cellspacing="0"
          cellpadding="0"
          style="padding: 0; margin: 0; border-collapse: collapse">
<tr style="padding: 0; margin: 0">
<td width="728"
      colspan="2"
      style="padding: 0; margin: 0"><img
          src="logo.gif"
          style="padding: 0; margin"></td>
</tr>
<tr style="padding: 0; margin: 0">
<td width="728"
      colspan="2"
      style="padding: 0; margin: 0"><div
        style="padding: 0;
                  margin: 0;
                  text-align: center;
                  font-size: small;
```

```
                        background-color: #99CCCC">
        Publisher Application
</div></td>
</tr>
<tr>
    <td rowspan="2"
            width="240"
            valign="top">
        <div style="height: 500px; padding: 20px; border-right: 3px dashed;
                        margin-right: 20px">
            <a href="list-news-items">List News Items</a><br/>
            <a href="create-news-item">Create News Item</a><br/>
            <a href="logout">Logout</a> <br/>
        </div>
    </td>
    <td width="488">
        <div style="margin-top: 12px; margin-bottom: 12 px">
```

Figure 13.6: top.inc

The banner in the the publisher application web pages comes from **an image file called logo.gif**. You should store this directly within the web folder of the publisher project.

```
        </div>
    </td>
</tr>
<tr>
    <td valign="top">
```

Figure 13.7: middle.inc

143

```
    </td>
  </tr>
</table>

</body>
</html>
```

Figure 13.8: bottom.inc

144

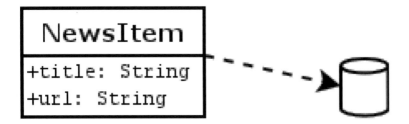

Figure 13.9: Initial Data Model For The Publisher Application

13.5   System Architecture

In this chapter, we continue building the publisher application with the data access object pattern described in the previous chapter on data access objects and the model-view-controller pattern described in the chapter on JSP.

A domain model is an object model of the domain that incorporates both behavior and data. In our case, the domain model consists of a single entity called NewsItem, which represents a news item to be Figure 13.9 shows the data model used in this chapter.

Initial data model for the publisher application

Figure 13.10 shows the various concerns within our application organized into a layered architecture. This architecture will form a basis for future iterations of the system in which we add functionality.

Layered architecture of the Publisher system

Actually, the architecture is not purely layered in the sense that elements of the presentation layer access elements of the persistence layer. In a strictly layered architecture, elements of the presentation layer would only be permitted to access elements of the business logic layer.

In the outermost layer, there is the user's web browser that makes TCP connections to the tomcat web container (also called a servlet/JSP container), through which it sends HTTP request messages.

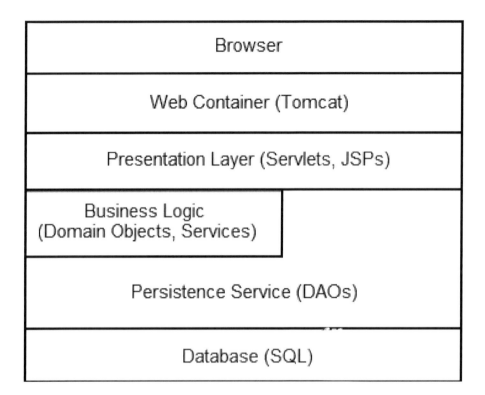

Figure 13.10: Publisher System Architecture

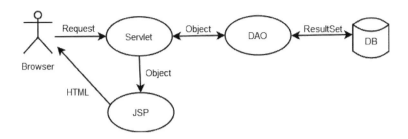

Figure 13.11: Architecture Based On Servlets JSP And Data Access Objects

The second layer is Tomcat, which parses incoming HTTP request messages into instances of the HttpSerlvetRequest class, and then passes these objects to the doGet or doPost methods of an appropriate servlet based on the request URL.

The third layer is the presentation layer, which is comprised of servlets and JSP scripts. The servlets act as controllers (request handlers) because their service methods (doGet, doPost) act as entry points into the web application. In response to user input, the servlets may lookup one or more business objects through the persistence layer and may invoke requested business functionality on them. After business functions have completed, the servlets invoke JSP scripts, passing to them references to appropriate domain objects. The purpose of the JSP is to generate the HTML to display to the user an appropriate view of the application state.

Some authors talk about a model-view-controller architecture in which servlets comprise the controller, JSP the view, and business logic the model.

The domain objects are plain old Java objects (POJOs) that model the data and behaviors of the (business) problem being solved. In our simple application, the business logic layer is comprised of instances of a class called NewsItem.

The persistence service is comprised of data access objects (DAOs). Recall that these classes are responsible for providing services needed to persist the application state as embodied in the domain objects. For each persistent domain object, there is a DAO; thus for our application, we have a single class called NewsItemDAO.

Finally, the database is situated on the lowest layer of the application. Reads and writes into the database will be performed by the methods in the DAOs. Figure 13.11 provides another illustration of the basic architecture that will be followed in this chapter.

13.6 Home Page

In this section, we add a home page for the publisher application. We implement the home page by defining a servlet that simply forwards requests to a jsp file.

There are several different sequences of activities we can take to implement the new functionality. In this section, we will use the following sequence.

1. Configure a new servlet in the deployment descriptor.

2. Implement the new servlet.

3. Implement the jsp.

4. Test.

Configure a new servlet in the deployment descriptor

Configure the home servlet by adding the following listing to the deployment descriptor.

```
<servlet>
    <servlet-name>home</servlet-name>
    <servlet-class>publisher.web.HomeServlet</servlet-class>
</servlet>
<servlet-mapping>
    <servlet-name>home</servlet-name>
    <url-pattern>/home</url-pattern>
</servlet-mapping>
```

Create HomeServlet

Create a servlet called HomeServlet in the publisher.web package from figure 13.12 listing.

```
package publisher.web;

import java.io.IOException;

import javax.servlet.RequestDispatcher;
import javax.servlet.ServletConfig;
```

```
import javax.servlet.ServletContext;
import javax.servlet.ServletException;
import javax.servlet.http.HttpServlet;
import javax.servlet.http.HttpServletRequest;
import javax.servlet.http.HttpServletResponse;

import org.apache.log4j.Logger;

public class HomeServlet extends HttpServlet {

    private Logger logger = Logger.getLogger(this.getClass());
    private RequestDispatcher jsp;

    public void init(ServletConfig config) throws ServletException {
        ServletContext context = config.getServletContext();
        jsp = context.getRequestDispatcher("/WEB-INF/jsp/home.jsp");
    }

    protected void doGet(HttpServletRequest req, HttpServletResponse resp)
    throws ServletException, IOException {
        logger.debug("home page requested");
        jsp.forward(req, resp);
    }
}
```

Figure 13.12: HomeServlet

Create JSP Files

Recall from the overview to this chapter that the JSP files will have the following structure.

```
<%@ include file="top.inc" %>
  <!-- page menu -->
<%@ include file="middle.inc" %>
  <!-- page content -->
<%@ include file="bottom.inc" %>
```

Now, we are ready to create the jsp file that the home servlet will forward to in order to generate the HTML. Create a file home.jsp inside the jsp folder with the contents of the following listing.

149

```
<%@ include file="top.inc" %>

<%@ include file="middle.inc" %>

<h1>Welcome</h1>

<p>
This is the publisher application.
It allows you to publish and manage a news feed.
</p>

<%@ include file="bottom.inc" %>
```

Because the home page has no page specific operations for the user, the section between the top and bottom includes is empty.

Test

Have Tomcat reprocess the web.xml file by stoping and starting the publisher application through the manager application and verify that the application is running correctly by going to the home page of the publisher application. Figure 13.13 shows approximately how the home page is rendered.

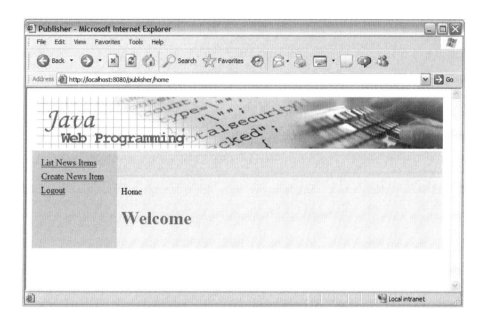

Figure 13.13: WelcomePage

13.7 List Page

Overview

In this section, we will implement the servlet and jsp to return the page that lists the news items in the system.

Modify the Deployment Descriptor

Modify the deployment descriptor, so that it uses the ListNewsItemsServlet to service requests that match the pattern */list-news-items*. The following listing shows the servlet elements for the list-news-items servlet.

```
<servlet>
    <servlet-name>list-news-items</servlet-name>
    <servlet-class>publisher.web.ListNewsItemsServlet</servlet-class>
</servlet>
<servlet-mapping>
    <servlet-name>list-news-items</servlet-name>
    <url-pattern>/list-news-items</url-pattern>
</servlet-mapping>
```

Create ListNewsItemsServlet

Create ListNewsItemsServlet in the publisher.web package with the implementation shown in figure 13.14.

Create JSP

Create list-news-items.jsp, and set its contents to figure 13.15 list.

Test

Stop and start the publisher application with the Tomcat manager application, so that Tomcat reloads the web.xml file and the new servlet. Verify that the the new functionality works correctly by going to **http://localhost:8080/ publisher/home** and following the link to the list items page. Figure 13.16 shows approximately how the list news items page should render.

```
package publisher.web;

import java.io.IOException;
import java.util.List;

import javax.servlet.RequestDispatcher;
import javax.servlet.ServletConfig;
import javax.servlet.ServletContext;
import javax.servlet.ServletException;
import javax.servlet.http.HttpServlet;
import javax.servlet.http.HttpServletRequest;
import javax.servlet.http.HttpServletResponse;

import org.apache.log4j.Logger;

import publisher.data.NewsItem;
import publisher.data.NewsItemDAO;

public class ListNewsItemsServlet extends HttpServlet
{
    private Logger logger = Logger.getLogger(this.getClass());
    private RequestDispatcher jsp;

    public void init(ServletConfig config) throws ServletException {
        ServletContext context = config.getServletContext();
        jsp = context.getRequestDispatcher("/WEB-INF/jsp/list-news-items.jsp");
    }


    protected void doGet(HttpServletRequest req, HttpServletResponse resp)
    throws ServletException, IOException
    {
        logger.debug("doGet()");
        List<NewsItem> newsItems = new NewsItemDAO().findAll();
        req.setAttribute("newsItems", newsItems);
        jsp.forward(req, resp);
    }
}
```

Figure 13.14: class ListNewsItemsServlet

153

```
<%@ page import="java.util.Iterator" %>
<%@ page import="publisher.data.NewsItem" %>
<jsp:useBean id="newsItems" scope="request" type="java.util.List" />
<%@ include file="top.inc" %>
    <a href="create-news-item">Create News Item</a>
<%@ include file="middle.inc" %>
<ul>
    <%
        Iterator it = newsItems.iterator();
        while (it.hasNext())
        {
            NewsItem newsItem = (NewsItem) it.next();
    %>
        <li>
            <a href="view-news-item?id=<%=newsItem.getId()%>"><%=newsItem.getTitle()%></a>
        </li>
    <% } %>
</ul>
<%@ include file="bottom.inc" %>
```

Figure 13.15: list-news-items.jsp

154

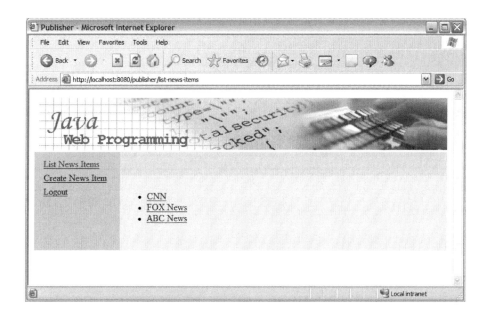

Figure 13.16: List News Items Page

Note that the links on the list items page will not work yet. In the next section we implement the view item page, so that the links to the news items in the list will bring the user to the view item page.

13.8 View Page

Overview

So far, we have created the functionality for a single page: the page that lets the user see a list of news items in the system. In this section, we will create functionality needed to display the details of a particular news item.

Look at the page flow diagram. We have finished the page to list items and we are starting to create the page to view an item. This page provides menu choices to edit or delete the news item being viewed.

Configure a New Servlet in the Deployment Descriptor

On the list news items page, we render each news item title as a hyperlink that invokes a servlet through the URL view-news-item?id=n, where n is the id of the news item. Therefore, we need to modify the web.xml to route requests that match this pattern to a serlvet that can return the desired page. To do this, add to the deployment descriptor the servlet and servlet-mapping elements shown in the following listing.

```
<servlet>
  <servlet-name>view-news-item</servlet-name>
  <servlet-class>publisher.web.ViewNewsItemServlet</servlet-class>
</servlet>
<servlet-mapping>
  <servlet-name>view-news-item</servlet-name>
  <url-pattern>/view-news-item</url-pattern>
</servlet-mapping>
```

Implement ViewNewsItemServlet

Create ViewNewsItemServlet with the contents of figure 13.17 listing.

```
package publisher.web;

import java.io.IOException;

import javax.servlet.RequestDispatcher;
import javax.servlet.ServletConfig;
import javax.servlet.ServletContext;
```

157

```
import javax.servlet.ServletException;
import javax.servlet.http.HttpServlet;
import javax.servlet.http.HttpServletRequest;
import javax.servlet.http.HttpServletResponse;

import org.apache.log4j.Logger;

import publisher.data.NewsItem;
import publisher.data.NewsItemDAO;

public class ViewNewsItemServlet extends HttpServlet
{
    private Logger logger = Logger.getLogger(this.getClass());
    private RequestDispatcher jsp;

    public void init(ServletConfig config) throws ServletException {
        ServletContext context = config.getServletContext();
        jsp = context.getRequestDispatcher("/WEB-INF/jsp/view-news-item.jsp");
    }

    protected void doGet(HttpServletRequest req, HttpServletResponse resp)
    throws ServletException, IOException
    {
        logger.debug("doGet()");
        String idString = req.getParameter("id");
        Long id = new Long(idString);
        NewsItem newsItem = new NewsItemDAO().find(id);
        req.setAttribute("newsItem", newsItem);
        jsp.forward(req, resp);
    }
}
```

Figure 13.17: ViewNewsItemServlet

Create JSP

Create view-news-item.jsp with the contents of figure 13.18 listing.

Test

Stop and start the publisher application with the Tomcat manager application so that Tomcat reloads the web.xml file and the new servlet. Verify that the new functionality

158

```
<%@ include file="top.inc" %>

   <a href="edit-news-item?id=${newsItem.id}">Edit</a>
   <a href="delete-news-item?id=${newsItem.id}">Delete</a>

<%@ include file="middle.inc" %>

<table>
   <tr>
      <td>Title:</td>
      <td>${newsItem.title}</td>

   </tr>
   <tr>
      <td>Url:</td>
      <td>
         ${newsItem.url}
         <a href="${newsItem.url}">test link</a>

      </td>
   </tr>
</table>

<%@ include file="bottom.inc" %>
```

Figure 13.18: view-news-item.jsp

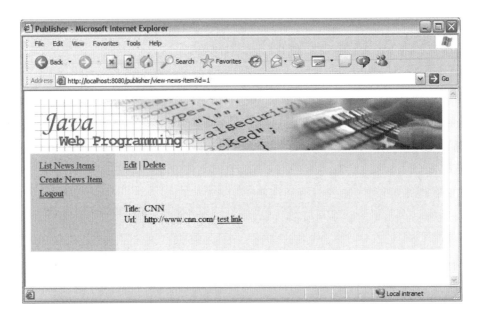

Figure 13.19: View news Item Page

works correctly by first going to the following url.

```
http://localhost:8080/publisher/home
```

Second, following the link to the list items page and then click on a title to go to the view item page for that news item. Figure 13.19 shows approximately how the view news item page should render.

160

13.9 Edit Page

Overview

In this section, we create functionality needed to edit the attributes of a particular news item. We will follow the same sequence of activities as previously followed to build the other servlets in this chapter, but with the addition of a step to modify the NewsItemDAO. The steps are as follows.

```
\item Add an update method to the news item DAO.
\item Configure a new servlet in the deployment descriptor.
\item Implement the new servlet.
\item Implement the jsp.
\item Test.
```

Editing a news item is a two step process for the user. First, the user requests the edit form for a selected news item. Second, the user submits the form. The first step of this process requires that an SQL select command be executed because the application needs to populate the edit form with the current state of the selected news item. The second step of this process requires execution of an SQL update command because the application needs to modify the state of the news item as represented in the database. In accordance with our DAO-based approach, we hide these details from the edit news item servlet. The form will be populated with data from an instance of NewsItem that we get from calling the find method of the news item DAO, and the state of the news item in the database will be updated through a call to the update method of the news item DAO.

The two-step process of retrieving the current value of the item and then changing it is referred to as a *business transaction*. Business transactions encompass one or more database transactions. In our case, our business transaction encompasses two database transactions: a read and a write. One issue with business transactions such as this one is how to handle inconsistent user input. For example, if person A goes to the edit page for a given news item and person B goes to the same page just a moment after A goes there, but before A submits changes, then both A and B see the same version of the news item. However, as soon as one person submits their changes, the other person will be making changes on the basis of stale information. When the second person submits their changes, they will overwrite the changes made by the first person without ever having seen those changes. It is possible that the two people are responsible for different things, and that these resposibilities have them modify

161

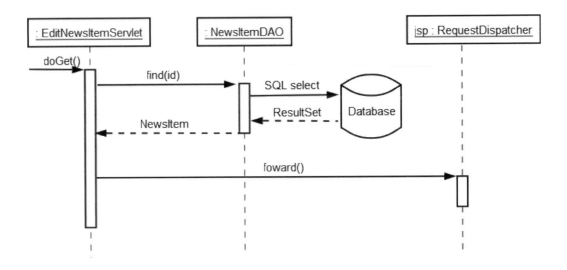

Figure 13.20: Sequence Diagram For Getting News item

two different fields of the news items. In this case, one person loses the results of their work. If these types of problems are a threat to the application, then strategies must be used to eliminate the problems. In this chapter we not consider this problem any further.

Figure 13.20 is a sequence diagram that illustrates the sequence of activities resulting from a request for the edit form for a news item, which is the first step in our two-step process.

When the user wishes to modify a news item, he or she first views the object through the view-news-item page. In this page, there is an edit link. When the user clicks the edit link, the browser will send an HTTP GET request for the following resource (assuming the selected NewsItem has an id equal to 3):

```
/edit-news-item?id=3
```

The doGet method of EditNewsItemServlet extracts the value of the id parameter, which is 3 in our example, and then passes this value to the find method of the news item DAO.

The servlet then stores a reference to the news item instance returned by the find method in the HttpServletRequest object (which acts as a container for request-

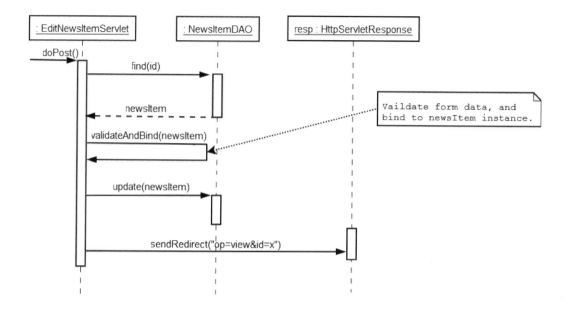

Figure 13.21: Sequence Diagram For Posting News item

specific data), and then invokes the forward method on an instance of the RequestDis-pathcer class that encapsulates the JSP that generates the HTML for the edit form. The edit-news-item JSP uses the properties of the news item instance to populate its form fields, so the user can modify the current state of the selected news item.

Figure 13.21 is a sequence diagram that illustrates the sequence of activities that result when the user submits changes to the news item edit form, which is the second step in the two-step business transaction.

After the user finishes making edits to the news item, the user clicks the submit button to save the changes. When this happens, the browser constructs an HTTP POST request message with the data from the form and sends it to the servlet container. The servlet container parses the request message into an instance of the HttpServletRequest class and passes this to the doPost method of the singleton instance of the EditNewsItemServlet class. The servlet container also passes an instance of HttpServletResponse, which is used to construct a response to be sent back to the browser.

The doPost method of the EditNewsItemServlet instance checks to see if the data entered by the user is valid (a process called validation), and if valid, invokes the

```
public void update(NewsItem newsItem)
{
   PreparedStatement statement = null;
   Connection connection = null;
   try
   {
      connection = getConnection();
      String sql = "update news_item set " + "title=?, url=? where id=?";
      statement = connection.prepareStatement(sql);
      statement.setString(1, newsItem.getTitle());
      statement.setString(2, newsItem.getUrl());
      statement.setLong(3, newsItem.getId().longValue());
      statement.execute();
   } catch (SQLException e)
   {
      throw new RuntimeException(e);
   } finally
   {
      close(statement, connection);
   }
}
```

Figure 13.22: update method

update method of the news item DAO to modify the attributes of the given news item according to the values entered by the user in the HTML form. After updating the database, the servlet redirects the browser to the view-news-item page, which causes the browser to submit a separate HTTP request to the web application to view the result of the edit operation.

Modify News Item DAO

Open the news item DAO class and add figure 13.22 implementation of the update method. As you can see, the update method issues an SQL update command to modify the state of a news item in the news item table. Note that it is possible that another user deleted the news item just prior to executing the update method. When this happens, the call to execute will throw an SQLException. We wrap the SQLException in a RuntimeException so that we can throw it to calling code with declaring the method with a throws clause. We can do this because RuntimeException is an *unchecked exception*. Throwing unchecked exceptions simplifies the code by avoid the need to explicitly throw or catch exceptions. Using unchecked exceptions is the current trend in programming style; all exception in C# for instance are unchecked.

The finally clause ensures that we call the close method regardless of whether an exception occurs. Remeber that closing database connections is essential when using database connection pooling. If we fail to close connection, we will exhaust the connection pool and threads will start blocking forever on calls for new connections.

Modify Deployment Descriptor

On the view news item page, we provide a menu choice to edit the news item being viewed. This link invokes the edit-news-item servlet through the URL edit-news-item?id=n, where n is the id of the news item. Therefore, you should modify web.xml to route requests that match this pattern to an instance of EditNewsItemSerlvet that is named edit-news-item. To do this, add the contents of the following listing to the deployment descriptor.

```
<servlet>
   <servlet-name>edit-news-item</servlet-name>
   <servlet-class>publisher.web.EditNewsItemServlet</servlet-class>
</servlet>
<servlet-mapping>
   <servlet-name>edit-news-item</servlet-name>
   <url-pattern>/edit-news-item</url-pattern>
</servlet-mapping>
```

Implement EditNewsItemServlet

Create EditNewsItemServlet with the contents of figure 13.23.

```
package publisher.web;

import java.io.IOException;
import java.util.HashMap;
import java.util.Map;

import javax.servlet.RequestDispatcher;
import javax.servlet.ServletConfig;
import javax.servlet.ServletContext;
import javax.servlet.ServletException;
import javax.servlet.http.HttpServlet;
```

165

```java
import javax.servlet.http.HttpServletRequest;
import javax.servlet.http.HttpServletResponse;

import org.apache.log4j.Logger;

import publisher.data.NewsItem;
import publisher.data.NewsItemDAO;

public class EditNewsItemServlet extends HttpServlet
{
    private Logger logger = Logger.getLogger(this.getClass());
    private RequestDispatcher jsp;

    public void init(ServletConfig config) throws ServletException {
        ServletContext context = config.getServletContext();
        jsp = context.getRequestDispatcher("/WEB-INF/jsp/edit-news-item.jsp");
    }

    protected void doGet(HttpServletRequest req, HttpServletResponse resp)
    throws ServletException, IOException {
        logger.debug("doGet()");
        String idString = req.getParameter("id");
        Long id = new Long(idString);
        NewsItem newsItem = new NewsItemDAO().find(id);
        req.setAttribute("newsItem", newsItem);
        jsp.forward(req, resp);
    }

    protected void doPost(HttpServletRequest req, HttpServletResponse resp)
    throws ServletException, IOException
    {
        String id = req.getParameter("id");

        // Check if cancel button was pressed.
        String cancelButton = req.getParameter("cancel-button");
        if (cancelButton != null)
        {
            logger.debug("cancel button pressed");
            resp.sendRedirect("view-news-item?id=" + id);
            return;
        }
        Map<String, String> errors = validate(req);
        if (!errors.isEmpty())
        {
            logger.debug("validation errors");
```

166

```
      jsp.forward(req, resp);
      return;
   }

   NewsItem newsItem = (NewsItem) req.getAttribute("newsItem");
   new NewsItemDAO().update(newsItem);
   resp.sendRedirect("view-news-item?id=" + id);
}

public static Map<String, String> validate(HttpServletRequest req)
{
   NewsItem newsItem = new NewsItem();
   HashMap<String, String> errors = new HashMap<String, String>();
   req.setAttribute("errors", errors);
   req.setAttribute("newsItem", newsItem);

   String idString = req.getParameter("id");
   if (idString != null && idString.length() > 0)
   {
      Long id = new Long(idString);
      newsItem.setId(id);
   }

   // title
   String title = req.getParameter("title");
   if (title == null || title.trim().length() == 0)
   {
      errors.put("title", "Title required.");
   }
   newsItem.setTitle(title);

   // url
   String url = req.getParameter("url");
   if (url == null || url.trim().length() == 0)
   {
      errors.put("url", "URL required.");
   }
   newsItem.setUrl(url);

   return errors;
   }
}
```

There are two ways the doPost methods will be called: the user clicks cancel or the user clicks submit. Accordingly, the doPost method first checks to see if the user

Figure 13.23: EditNewsItemServlet

clicked on cancel. If the user clicked cancel, then the doPost method will redirect the browser back to the view-news-item page. If the user clicked submit, then doPost will check to see that the data entered by the user is valid, which it does by calling the validate method.

The validate method is implemented as a static method because it will also be called from the doPost method of the servlet that will be used to handle requests to create news items. By placing the code in its own method that can be externally invoked, we keep the validation code in a single location and avoid creating duplicate code.

The validate method returns a map that contains an entry for each validation error that is detected. Therefore, the doPost method checks to see if any validation errors occurred by checking to see if this map is empty. If the map is not empty, then it forwards processing of the request to the jsp with the edit form, which will display the data entered by the user in the form along with the error messages. If there are no entries in the errors map, then doPost will consider the data submission to be valid and will then proceed to store the new values in the database.

The validate method extracts the title and url attributes from the request parameters. It checks to see if the values submitted by the user are valid. If a submitted value is invalid, the validate method adds an entry in a map called errors. The errors map associates a parameter in the form with a validation error message, and it is returned by the validate method. In addition to checking for validation errors, the validate method has a side effect: it stores the values of the parameters as attributes in the request object. The reason for doing this is that if there are validation errors, then the calling code will forward the request to the jsp with the form; the jsp needs access to the values the user submitted in order to echo them back to the user.

Create JSP

Create edit-news-item.jsp with the contents of figure 13.24.

```
<jsp:useBean id="errors" scope="request" type="java.util.Map"
            class="java.util.HashMap" />

<%@ include file="top.inc" %>
<%@ include file="middle.inc" %>
```

```
<form method="post">
   <table>
      <tr>
         <td>Title</td>
         <td><input type="text" name="title" value="${newsItem.title}" size="50" />
            <%
               if (errors.containsKey("title")) {
                  out.println("<span class=\"error\">" + errors.get("title") +
         "</span>");
               }
            %>
         </td>
      </tr>
      <tr>
         <td>URL</td>
         <td><input type="text" name="url" value="${newsItem.url}" size="50" />
            <%
               if (errors.containsKey("url")) {
                  out.println("<span class=\"error\">" + errors.get("url") +
         "</span>");
               }
            %>
         </td>
      </tr>
      <tr>
         <td>
            <input type="submit" name="submit-button" value="Submit" />
            <input type="submit" name="cancel-button" value="Cancel" />
         </td>
      </tr>
   </table>
   <input type="hidden" name="id" value="${newsItem.id}" />

</form>

<%@ include file="bottom.inc" %>
```

Figure 13.24: edit-news-item.jsp

Notice how field-specific error messages are displayed next to their fields.

169

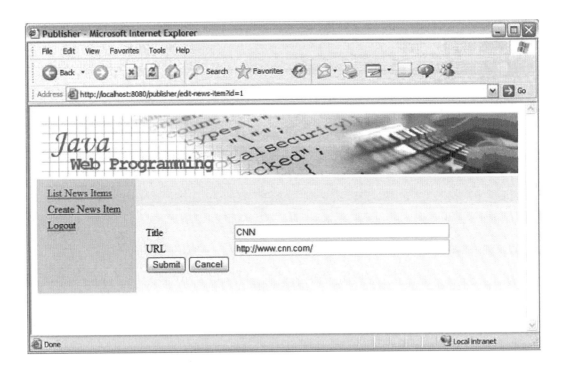

Figure 13.25: Edit News Item Page

Test

Stop and start the publisher application with the Tomcat manager application so that Tomcat reloads the web.xml file and the new class files. Verify that the new functionality works correctly by first going to the following url.

```
http://localhost:8080/publisher/home
```

Second, edit an existing news item. You should try entering in an empty title and an empty url to see how validation works. Figure 13.25 shows approximately how the edit news item page should render.

```
public void create(NewsItem newsItem)
{
    Long id = getUniqueId();
    newsItem.setId(id);
    PreparedStatement statement = null;
    Connection connection = null;
    try
    {
        connection = getConnection();
        String sql = "insert into news_item " + "(id, title, url) "
                + "values (?, ?, ?)";
        statement = connection.prepareStatement(sql);
        statement.setLong(1, id.longValue());
        statement.setString(2, newsItem.getTitle());
        statement.setString(3, newsItem.getUrl());
        statement.executeUpdate();
    } catch (SQLException e)
    {
        throw new RuntimeException(e);
    } finally
    {
        close(statement, connection);
    }
}
```

Figure 13.26: create method

13.10 Create Page

Overview

In this section, we will add functionality to enable the user to create additional news items. The logic needed for this task is similar to that used for the edit news item page.

Modify the news item DAO

Add figure 13.26 create method to the news item DAO.

The create method takes an instance of the NewsItem class and inserts a row in the news_item table to represent this instance. The create method generates a unique id to serve as a primary key for the newly inserted news item. It sets the id field

171

of the NewsItem object passed into it, so that the calling code has access to this newly generated value. It is possible to have MySQL generate a unique id as part of the insert command. This is done by declaring the id column with *auto_increment* during table creation. However, this feature is not part of standard SQL and is not implemented in all relational database servers. To keep the code portable to these other servers, we choose to generate our own primary keys.

Modify the Deployment Descriptor

Add configuration to web.xml so that CreateNewsItemServlet is invoked for requests matching /create-news-item as shown in the following listing.

```
<servlet>
    <servlet-name>create-news-item</servlet-name>
    <servlet-class>publisher.web.CreateNewsItemServlet</servlet-class>
</servlet>
<servlet-mapping>
    <servlet-name>create-news-item</servlet-name>
    <url-pattern>/create-news-item</url-pattern>
</servlet-mapping>
```

Create CreateNewsItemServlet

Create CreateNewsItemServlet with the contents of figure 13.27.

```
package publisher.web;

import java.io.IOException;
import java.util.Map;

import javax.servlet.RequestDispatcher;
import javax.servlet.ServletConfig;
import javax.servlet.ServletContext;
import javax.servlet.ServletException;
import javax.servlet.http.HttpServlet;
import javax.servlet.http.HttpServletRequest;
import javax.servlet.http.HttpServletResponse;

import org.apache.log4j.Logger;

import publisher.data.NewsItem;
```

172

```
import publisher.data.NewsItemDAO;

public class CreateNewsItemServlet extends HttpServlet
{
    private Logger logger = Logger.getLogger(this.getClass());
    private RequestDispatcher jsp;

    public void init(ServletConfig config) throws ServletException {
        ServletContext context = config.getServletContext();
        jsp = context.getRequestDispatcher("/WEB-INF/jsp/edit-news-item.jsp");
    }

    protected void doGet(HttpServletRequest req, HttpServletResponse resp)
    throws ServletException, IOException
    {
        logger.debug("doGet()");
        jsp.forward(req, resp);
    }

    protected void doPost(HttpServletRequest req, HttpServletResponse resp)
    throws ServletException, IOException
    {
        // Check if cancel button was pressed.
        String cancelButton = req.getParameter("cancel-button");
        if (cancelButton != null)
        {
            logger.debug("cancel button pressed");
            resp.sendRedirect("list-news-items");
            return;
        }
        Map<String, String> errors = EditNewsItemServlet.validate(req);
        if (!errors.isEmpty())
        {
            logger.debug("validation errors");
            jsp.forward(req, resp);
            return;
        }

        NewsItem newsItem = (NewsItem) req.getAttribute("newsItem");
        new NewsItemDAO().create(newsItem);
        resp.sendRedirect("view-news-item?id=" + newsItem.getId());
    }
}
```

Figure 13.27: CreateNewsItemServlet

In the doPost method, the first thing we do is check for the cancel button. If pressed, we send the user to the list-news-items page.

If the cancel button was not pressed, we validate and bind form data to an instance of NewsItem. If there are validation errors, we pass the newsItem and errors objects to the jsp to display the user input and the validation error messages.

Validation and binding for object creation and object editing are identical. For this reason, we invoke validate in EditNewsItemServlet, rather than replicate the code in CreateNewsItem. For this to work, we declared the validateAndBind method of EditNewsItemServlet as static.

If there are no validation errors, we invoke the create method of the NewsItemDAO class. Unlike EditNewsItemServlet, we don't need to worry about NotFoundException.

After creating the news item in the database, we return the user to the view-news-item page, so that he can verify that the news item was created. (Alternatively, we could have redirected the user to the list-news-items page.) The create method of NewsItemDAO has the side effect of setting the id attribute of the NewsItem object passed into it. For this reason, we are able to redirect the user to the view news item page with the id of the newly created news item.

Test

Stop and start the publisher application with the Tomcat manager application so that Tomcat reloads the web.xml file and the new class files. Verify that the new functionality works correctly by first going to the following url.

```
http://localhost:8080/publisher/home
```

Second, create an additional news item. You should try entering in an empty title and an empty url to check that validation works correctly. Figure 13.28 shows approximately how the create news item page should render.

174

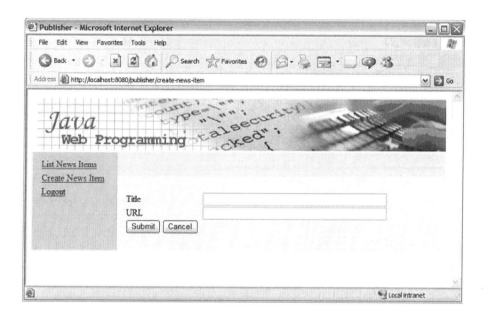

Figure 13.28: Create News Item Page

13.11 Delete Page

Overview

In this section, we will add functionality to enable the user to delete news items. The logic need for this task is similar to that used for the edit news item page.

Modify the news item DAO

Add figure 13.29 implementation of the delete method to the news item DAO.

```java
public void delete(NewsItem newsItem)
{
    PreparedStatement statement = null;
    Connection connection = null;
    try
    {
        connection = getConnection();
        String sql = "delete from news_item where id=?";
        statement = connection.prepareStatement(sql);
        Long id = newsItem.getId();
        statement.setLong(1, id.longValue());
        statement.executeUpdate();
    } catch (SQLException e)
    {
        throw new RuntimeException(e);
    } finally
    {
        close(statement, connection);
    }
}
```

Figure 13.29: delete method

The delete method takes a news item instance as its sole argument. However, the delete method only needs the id attribute within the news item instance, which it uses within the where clause of an SQL delete command. Note that like the update method, it is possible that some other user deleted the object just prior to the execution of this delete method. However, in this case we silently ignore this unexpected scenario, because the user intends to delete the news item anyway. However, the application

176

would give the user the impression that he or she deleted the news item rather that
it being first deleted by someone else. If this false impression were to have negative
consequences in some application scenario, then we would change the behavior of the
delete method by throwing a NotFoundException in order to inform calling code of
the abnormal completeion of the operation.

Modify the Deployment Descriptor

Add configuration to web.xml so that DeleteNewsItemServlet is invoked for requests
matching /delete-news-item as the following listing.

```
<servlet>
    <servlet-name>delete-news-item</servlet-name>
    <servlet-class>publisher.web.DeleteNewsItemServlet</servlet-class>
</servlet>
<servlet-mapping>
    <servlet-name>delete-news-item</servlet-name>
    <url-pattern>/delete-news-item</url-pattern>
</servlet-mapping>
```

Create DeleteNewsItemServlet

Create DeleteNewsItemServlet by using the contents of figure 13.30.

```
package publisher.web;

import java.io.IOException;

import javax.servlet.RequestDispatcher;
import javax.servlet.ServletConfig;
import javax.servlet.ServletContext;
import javax.servlet.ServletException;
import javax.servlet.http.HttpServlet;
import javax.servlet.http.HttpServletRequest;
import javax.servlet.http.HttpServletResponse;

import org.apache.log4j.Logger;

import publisher.data.NewsItem;
import publisher.data.NewsItemDAO;
```

177

```
public class DeleteNewsItemServlet extends HttpServlet
{
    private Logger logger = Logger.getLogger(this.getClass());
    private RequestDispatcher jsp;

    public void init(ServletConfig config) throws ServletException {
        ServletContext context = config.getServletContext();
        jsp = context.getRequestDispatcher("/WEB-INF/jsp/delete-news-item.jsp");
    }

    protected void doGet(HttpServletRequest req, HttpServletResponse resp)
    throws ServletException, IOException
    {
        logger.debug("doGet()");
        jsp.forward(req, resp);
    }

    protected void doPost(HttpServletRequest req, HttpServletResponse resp)
    throws ServletException, IOException
    {
        String idString = req.getParameter("id");

        // Check if cancel button was pressed.
        String cancelButton = req.getParameter("cancel-button");
        if (cancelButton != null)
        {
            logger.debug("cancel button pressed");
            resp.sendRedirect("view-news-item?id=" + idString);
            return;
        }

        NewsItemDAO newsItemDAO = new NewsItemDAO();
        Long id = new Long(idString);
        NewsItem newsItem = newsItemDAO.find(id);
        new NewsItemDAO().delete(newsItem);
        resp.sendRedirect("list-news-items");
    }
}
```

Figure 13.30: DeleteNewsItemServlet

The first thing we do inside doPost is to check for the cancel button. If pressed, we redirect the user to the view-news-item page so that he can verify that the news

```
<%@ include file="top.inc" %>
<%@ include file="middle.inc" %>

<p>
Are you sure you want to delete this news item?
</p>

<form method="post">
   <input type="submit" name="delete-button" value="Delete" />
   <input type="submit" name="cancel-button" value="Cancel" />
   <input type="hidden" name="id" value="${params['id']}" />

</form>

<%@ include file="bottom.inc" %>
```

Figure 13.31: delete-news-item.jsp

item has not been deleted.

If the cancel button was not pressed, we perform a find on the news item because we have designed the DAO delete method to take a NewsItem object. In case another user deleted the news item already, we check to make sure the news item is not null. If not null, we pass it to the delete method of NewsItemDAO.

Finally, we redirect the user to the list-news-items page so that he can verify that the news item was deleted.

Create the JSP

Create delete-news-item.jsp with the contents of figure 13.31. Notice that we pass the id of the news item through a hidden input element.

Test

Stop and start the publisher application with the Tomcat manager application so that Tomcat reloads the web.xml file and the new class files. Verify that the new functionality works correctly by first going to the following url.

```
http://localhost:8080/publisher/home
```

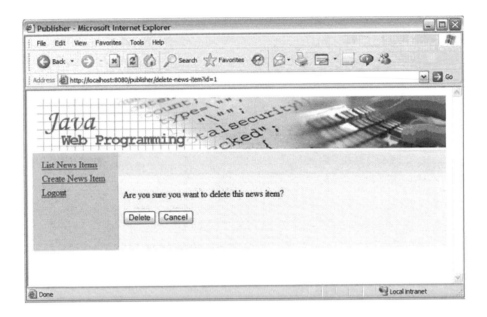

Figure 13.32: Delete Page

Second, delete a news item. You should also verify that the cancel operation works correctly. Figure 13.32 shows approximately how the create news item page should render.

13.12 Exercises

1. Add link to list items page

Modify the list-news-item page, so that the url of the news item is displayed along with the news item title.

2. Bad item id

Enter the URL **http://localhost:8080/publisher/view-news-item?id=9999** into your browser and observe what happens. In our code we do not handle the case when the news item servlet receives a request with an invalid news item id. Change the news item servlet so that when an invalid news item id is received, the user is redirected to the list-news-item page. The following statement shows how to redirect the browser to the list news items page.

```
resp.sendRedirect("list-news-items");
```

3. Multi-user problems

In the previous exercise, you looked at how a user can deliberately input invalid data to make the application malfunction. However, it is possible that the web application malfunctions in the same way in another scenario in which the user is not trying to deliberately break the system. Explain the scenario in which the user innocently clicks on a news item link in the list-news-item page and is sent to the view-news-item page with an invalid id. (Hint: the scenario requires that there are at least two users logged in at the same time, or that one user is logged in with the same username in two different browser instances.)

Carry out the scenario you describe in order to verify that your answer is correct.

4. Reducing code duplication through inheritance

Re-organize the architecture of the system by creating a ParentServlet that all other servlets extend and move common functionality into the parent class. In particular, move the jsp variable, dataSource variable, and close method into ParentServlet. (Change the modifier from private to protected so that these can be accessed by subclasses.)

181

5. Servlet initialization parameters

This exercise assumes you have completed the previous exercise. Eliminate the init method from all of your servlets and create a single init method in ParentServlet. This init method will set the jsp path from an initialization parameter passed into it through the web.xml file.

In the web.xml file, modify the servlet declarations in order to pass in an initialization parameter called jsp. The jsp initialization parameter should be accessed inside the init method of ParentServlet. To carry out this exercise, you will need to perform research to find out how to do two things:

- how to specify an initialization parameter for a servlet in the deployment descriptor (web.xml)

- how to access the value of the initialization parameter in the init method

6. Graceful user error handling

Consider the following scenario. Suppose user A obtains an edit form for a particular NewsItem and then user B deletes this newsItem. When A submits changes to this news item, the EditNewsItemServlet will call the update method of NewsItemDAO, which issues an SQL update command to the database. This update command will fail because a record with the given id will not exist in the news_item table.

Modify the application so that it handles this situation gracefully in the following manner. In the publisher.data package, create a class called NotFoundException that extends the Exception class. Throw this exception from within the update method of the DAOs when a servlet tries to update an object that doesn't exist in the database. (You should simply create a class called NotFoundException that extends Exception; you do not need to implement any methods in this class.)

In the EditNewsItemServlet, if NotFoundException is thrown, then set a message attribute in the request object and forward to the home jsp. In the home jsp, look for the presence of the message attribute and display it if present. This will also serve as a means to inform the user of other possible abnormal conditions. The following lines of code can be added to home.jsp to accomplish this.

182

```
<%
    String message = (String) request.getAttribute("message");
    if (message != null) {
            out.println("<p>" + message + "</p>");
    }
%>
```

Before implementing the solution to this problem, carry out the senario to set how the application malfunctions.

Chapter 14

Web Application Security

14.1 Objectives

- Learn the ways in which web applications are made secure

- Learn how to generate public/private key pairs and store them in a key store

- Learn how to generate a self-signed certificate

- Learn how to configure Tomcat to support https

- Learn how authentication works in web applications

- Learn how to add authentication to web application

- Learn how to add authorization to a web application

- Learn how to generate and use password digests

14.2 Overview

Web applications are made secure in the following ways:

- The environment in which the web application executes is made secure. This is sometimes referred to as *system hardening*. This is a system administration topic and is not covered in this book.

- HTTP exchanges between browser and server take place within the SSL/TLS communications protocol. The combined use of both protocols is referred to as HTTPS.

- Users identify themselves to the application by submitting a username and password; the server identifies itself to connecting browsers with the use of the public key infrastructure (PKI). These two procedures are referred to as user authentication and server authentication, respectively.

- Authorization to access web application resources — identified by the resource component of the URL — is enforced according to a security policy.

- Data submitted into the web application from connecting clients is validated before being accepted.

The list presented above is the foundation of web application security; however, it does not cover all security concerns. For a more complete list of issues and measures to take, consult other sources.

14.3 Configuration of HTTPS

Overview

These instructions explain how to configure Tomcat for SSL/TLS. After following these instructions, users may access web applications securely through port 8443.

The instructions show how to generate a self-signed certificate that browsers can use to authenticate the server. Consequently, browsers will not be able verify the authenticity of the certificate because it will not have been signed by a trusted third party whose certificates are pre-installed in the client system or added to the client system. For a commercial web site open to the public, you would typically have a third party sign your certificate and use this to authenticate yourself to browsers. For a web application that is intended to be used by a pre-defined group of users, you can avoid purchasing signed certificate by adding your self-signed certificate to the trust stores within the client environments.

You can still use HTTPS without doing any of the above procedures, but your users will need to accept an untrusted certificate each time they visit your site. The following instructions show how to setup your system in this way.

Create Keystore with Self-Signed Certificate

In this section you will generate a self-signed certificate and store it in a file called *keystore* under the *conf* folder within the Tomcat system. You will then configure Tomcat to use this keystore to access to certifate and its corresponding private key needed to establish HTTPS connections.

We will generate the key pair and certificate with the keytool command, which is part of the Java SDK. In chapter 2, you were instructed to install the Java Development Kit (JDK). However, until this point you only needed the Java Runtime Environment (JRE), so this is the first instance where you need a tool from the JDK. If you did not install the JDK, then you should do so now to get access to the keytool command.

It's possible to run the keytool command as needed on a single line entered at the command prompt of the operating system. It's also possible to create a script that executes the command for you when you run the script. These script files are character-based files that you create in a text editor, such as Wordpad on Windows. Under Windows, you create a *batch* file to run commands from a file rather than typing them into the command line. Figure 14.1 shows how the command might be written in a Windows batch file. The caret symbol (^) at the end of each line

```
keytool -genkey ^
        -keystore keystore ^
        -alias tomcat ^
        -keyalg RSA ^
        -keysize 2048 ^
        -dname CN=localhost ^
        -storepass changeit ^
        -keypass changeit
```

Figure 14.1: Running keytool under Windows

```
keytool -genkey \
        -keystore keystore \
        -alias tomcat \
        -keyalg RSA \
        -keysize 2048 \
        -dname CN=localhost \
        -storepass changeit \
        -keypass changeit
```

Figure 14.2: Running keytool under Linux

indicates line continuation. You can omit the line continuation character if you want to have all of the command occupy a single line.

Figure 14.2 shows how the keytool command would be written in a Linux shell script. Note that the line continuation character under Linux is a slash rather than a caret symbol. Under Linux, you would normally store the command in a file with extension .sh. Also, you may need to change the file permissions of the file to make it executable. If the file were called *gencert.sh*, then you could run the following command to make it executable.

```
chmod +x gencert.sh
```

After creating the script to execute the keytool command as needed, you should run the script. Under Windows, just enter the name of the batch file. For instance, if the file were called *gencert.bat*, then enter the following.

188

```
gencert.bat
```

Note: the keeytoll command may take a long time to complete, so be patient. If you get a message that the command is unknown, then you need to provide the full pathname to the keytool executable (or add the bin folder in your JDK installation to the path variable in your environment).

Under Linux, you may need to prefix the script name with the current directory if the current directory is not in your system path. This would be done as follows.

```
.\gencert.sh
```

Once again, this command may take a long time to complete, so let it run for several minutes if necessary.

In the above commands, we leave the storepass and keypass values both equal to *changeit*. If you change these to other values, you may need to do additional configuration to get the system working, so it is simplier at this point to leave these values as *changeit*.

After the command completes, you should move the resulting keystore file into Tomcat's conf folder. Under Windows, you may need to be administrator to write the keystore file into Tomcat's conf folder.

The *CN* variable in the certificate should contain the domain name of your server. Because you are running Tomcat and the browser from the same machine, setting the *CN* variable to *localhost* as done above is OK. However, if you wanted to access Tomcat from a remote machine, you would need to replace *localhost* with the domain name (or IP address) of the machine on which Tomcat is running.

Configuring Tomcat

Uncomment the Connector element in `${TOMCAT_HOME}\conf\server.xml` that has a port attribute set to 8443. Also, add a *keystoreFile* attribute to this element as follows.

```
keystoreFile="conf/keystore"
```

Figure 14.3 is an example Connector element that sets up HTTPS on port 8443.

```
<Connector port="8443"
          maxThreads="200"
          minSpareThreads="5"
          maxSpareThreads="75"
          enableLookups="true"
          disableUploadTimeout="true"
          acceptCount="100"
          scheme="https"
          secure="true"
          SSLEnabled="true"
          clientAuth="false"
          sslProtocol="TLS"
          keystorePass="changeit"
          keystoreFile="conf/keystore" />
```

Figure 14.3: HTTPS Connector Element

If the above configuration fails for you, it may be that you changed the passwords from *changeit* to some other value when you ran keytool. In this case, add the following attribute to the above connector element, where storepass-value is the value of your trust store password and keypass-value is the value of your keystore password.

```
truststorepass="storepass-value"
keystorePass="keypass-value"
```

If you are running Windows, regular users may not have the privileges to modify server.xml. In this case, you need to edit server.xml as adminstrator. To do this, right click on wordpad in the Windows start menu and select *run as adminstrator*.

Test

Test your configuration by starting — or restarting — Tomcat and pointing your browser to **https://localhost:8443/publisher/home**. A security alert is presented to you because the browser you are using does not contain in its trust store the certificate you generated that Tomcat is using; the certificate is used by Tomcat, not by the browser. What is typically done is that the certificate you generate is submitted to a certificate signing authority, such as Verisign or Entrust, which then generates a publicly available certificate that contains your certificate and their sign of approval. Your browser has pre-installed within it the root certificates used by the commonly used certificate signing companies, which it uses to verify the authenticity of your certificate. When this is done, the browser will not generate a warning.

Note that if you want to change the port number used for HTTPS, make sure you change the redirect attribute of the unencrypted connector element in server.xml to your new value.

14.4   The Persistent User Class

When users login into the application they provide a username and password. The web application will look up the username in the database and check to see if the username exists, and if so, it will check to see if the supplied password matches the one in the database. For this purpose, we create a User class and its corresponding data access object (DAO); see Figure 14.4.

```
package publisher.data;

public class User {
        private Long id;
        private String username;
        private String password;

        public Long getId() {
                return id;
        }

        public void setId(Long id) {
                this.id = id;
        }

        public String getPassword() {
                return password;
        }

        public void setPassword(String password) {
                this.password = password;
        }

        public String getUsername() {
                return username;
        }

        public void setUsername(String username) {
                this.username = username;
        }
}
```

Figure 14.4: The User Class

192

The User class contains member variables to store the id, username and password. Figure 14.5 contains the complete listing for the data access object class used to manage instances of the User class.

```java
package publisher.data;

import java.sql.Connection;
import java.sql.PreparedStatement;
import java.sql.ResultSet;
import java.sql.SQLException;
import java.util.LinkedList;
import java.util.List;

public class UserDAO extends DataAccessObject {
   private static UserDAO instance = new UserDAO();

   public static UserDAO getInstance() {
      return instance;
   }

   private User read(ResultSet rs) throws SQLException
   {
      Long id = new Long(rs.getLong("id"));
      String username = rs.getString("username");
      String password = rs.getString("password");
      User user = new User();
      user.setId(id);
      user.setUsername(username);
      user.setPassword(password);
      return user;
   }

   public User find(Long id)
   {
      ResultSet rs = null;
      PreparedStatement statement = null;
      Connection connection = null;
      try
      {
         connection = getConnection();
         String sql = "select * from user where id=?";
         statement = connection.prepareStatement(sql);
         statement.setLong(1, id.longValue());
         rs = statement.executeQuery();
         if (!rs.next())
```

```
      {
          return null;
      }
      return read(rs);
   }
   catch (SQLException e)
   {
      throw new RuntimeException(e);
   }
   finally
   {
      close(rs, statement, connection);
   }
}

public User findByUsername(String username)
{
   ResultSet rs = null;
   PreparedStatement statement = null;
   Connection connection = null;
   try
   {
      connection = getConnection();
      String sql = "select * from user where username=?";
      statement = connection.prepareStatement(sql);
      statement.setString(1, username);
      rs = statement.executeQuery();
      if (!rs.next())
      {
          return null;
      }
      return read(rs);
   }
   catch (SQLException e)
   {
      throw new RuntimeException(e);
   }
   finally
   {
      close(rs, statement, connection);
   }
}

public List<User> findAll()
{
```

```
   LinkedList<User> users = new LinkedList<User>();
   ResultSet rs = null;
   PreparedStatement statement = null;
   Connection connection = null;
   try
   {
      connection = getConnection();
      String sql = "select * from user order by id";
      statement = connection.prepareStatement(sql);
      rs = statement.executeQuery();
      while (rs.next())
      {
         User user = read(rs);
         users.add(user);
      }
      return users;
   }
   catch (SQLException e)
   {
      throw new RuntimeException(e);
   }
   finally
   {
      close(rs, statement, connection);
   }
}

public void update(User user)
{
   PreparedStatement statement = null;
   Connection connection = null;
   try
   {
      connection = getConnection();
      String sql = "update user set " + "password=? where id=?";
      statement = connection.prepareStatement(sql);
      statement.setString(1, user.getPassword());
      statement.setLong(2, user.getId().longValue());
      statement.executeUpdate();
   } catch (SQLException e)
   {
      throw new RuntimeException(e);
   } finally
   {
      close(statement, connection);
```

```java
    }
}

public void create(User user)
{
    Long id = getUniqueId();
    user.setId(id);
    PreparedStatement statement = null;
    Connection connection = null;
    try
    {
        connection = getConnection();
        String sql = "insert into user " + "(id, username, password) "

                + "values (?, ?, ?)";
        statement = connection.prepareStatement(sql);
        statement.setLong(1, id.longValue());
        statement.setString(2, user.getUsername());
        statement.setString(3, user.getPassword());
        statement.executeUpdate();
    } catch (SQLException e)
    {
        throw new RuntimeException(e);
    } finally
    {
        close(statement, connection);
    }
}

public void delete(User user)
{
    PreparedStatement statement = null;
    Connection connection = null;
    try
    {
        connection = getConnection();
        String sql = "delete from user where id=?";
        statement = connection.prepareStatement(sql);
        Long id = user.getId();
        statement.setLong(1, id.longValue());
        statement.executeUpdate();
    } catch (SQLException e)
    {
        throw new RuntimeException(e);
    } finally
```

```
    {
        close(statement, connection);
    }
  }
}
```

Figure 14.5: The UserDAO Class

The above implementation of the user DAO enables management of user accounts similar to the management of NewsItems. However, for the purpose of developing login and logout functionality, we only need the method findByUserName.

The following SQL command creates a table called user that can hold instances of the user class. You should add this to the createdb.sql script in the publisher project.

```
create table user
(
    id integer primary key,
    username varchar(255) unique,
    password varchar(255)
);
```

In order to get some user accounts for testing, add a few insert commands to the insertdb.sql script. The following is an example.

```
insert into user (id, username, password) values (4, 'admin', 'admin');
```

Modify the cleandb.sql script as well to delete the user table. Run the database scripts to rebuild the publisher database with user account information. Make sure that the ant build scripts run without error. Also, use the mysql command line client to verify that the database is recreated correctly.

197

14.5 Login Functionality

How Authentication Works

Communication between browsers and servers is done by exchanging messages in which the browser initiates the exchange by sending an HTTP request message and the server responds by returning an HTTP response message. Separate messages are tied together with the use of a session identifier, which is normally accomplished by the use of HTTP cookies. When the browser sends its first request message to the server, the server returns a Set-Cookie header in its HTTP response message that contains a session identifier. In subsequent requests, the browser returns the session identifier within an HTTP Cookie header.

On the server side, the session identifier is stored internally by Tomcat. You can associate objects with this identifier by accessing the Session object for the client. This is done by calling **getSession()** on the HttpServletRequest object that is passed into the **doGet() or doPost()** methods of your servlets. You associate objects with sessions by storing a name/value pair within the session, which acts like a map data structure. In this book, we represent the state of being logged in by storing the id of the logged in user in the session object for that user. When a request comes in for a protected resource, we look for this id in the session object; if we find an id, then we know that the user has already logged in.

Login Servlet

Add the following lines to the deployment descriptor in order to configure the login servlet into the application.

```
<servlet>
    <servlet-name>login</servlet-name>
    <servlet-class>publisher.web.LoginServlet</servlet-class>
</servlet>

<servlet-mapping>
    <servlet-name>login</servlet-name>
    <url-pattern>/login</url-pattern>
</servlet-mapping>
```

Create a class called LoginServlet that extends HttpServlet to handle requests for the login page and requests to process submission of login credentials. Figure 14.6 is an example LoginServlet that will suit our needs.

198

```
package publisher.web;

import java.io.IOException;

import javax.servlet.RequestDispatcher;
import javax.servlet.ServletConfig;
import javax.servlet.ServletContext;
import javax.servlet.ServletException;
import javax.servlet.http.HttpServlet;
import javax.servlet.http.HttpServletRequest;
import javax.servlet.http.HttpServletResponse;
import javax.servlet.http.HttpSession;

import org.apache.log4j.Logger;

import publisher.data.User;
import publisher.data.UserDAO;

public class LoginServlet extends HttpServlet {
    private Logger logger = Logger.getLogger(this.getClass());
    private RequestDispatcher jsp;

    public void init(ServletConfig config) throws ServletException {
        ServletContext context = config.getServletContext();
        jsp = context.getRequestDispatcher("/WEB-INF/jsp/login.jsp");
     }

    protected void doGet(HttpServletRequest req, HttpServletResponse resp)
    throws ServletException, IOException {
        logger.debug("doGet()");
        jsp.forward(req, resp);
    }

    protected void doPost(HttpServletRequest req, HttpServletResponse resp)
    throws ServletException, IOException {
        logger.debug("doPost()");

        String username = req.getParameter("username");
        User user = new UserDAO().findByUsername(username);
        if (user == null)
        {
            logger.debug("authentication failed: bad username");
            req.setAttribute("message", "Authentication failed.");
            jsp.forward(req, resp);
            return;
```

199

```
    }

    String password = req.getParameter("password");
    if (password == null || !user.getPassword().equals(password))
    {
        logger.debug("authentication failed: bad password");
        req.setAttribute("message", "Authentication failed.");
        jsp.forward(req, resp);
        return;
    }

    HttpSession session = req.getSession();
    Long userId = user.getId();
    session.setAttribute("userId", userId);
    logger.debug("authenticated");
    String url = "home";
    resp.sendRedirect(url);
    }
}
```

Figure 14.6: class LoginServlet

The init method in the login servlet stores a reference to the request dispatcher that is used to forward processing to the login jsp file. The doGet method simply forwards processing to the jsp through the request discpatcher.

The doPost method runs when the user submits the login form. The login form has two input fields: one named *username* and the other named *password*. The first thing the doPost method does is to get the username entered by the user (with a call to getAttribute on the request object), and then tries to retrieve the persistent User object with this username. If such a user object does not exist, the findByUsername method returns a null value. In case of a null value, doPost sets a message attribute in the request object and then forwards to the login jsp so that the login form is re-displayed to the user. However, this time, the user also sees a message saying that the authentication has failed. The jsp file got this failure message from the message attribute stored within the request object.

Note that after forwarding to the jsp, we return from the doPost method. It is a common mistake to forget to do this. If you do make this mistake, the servlet will continue processing the request after the jsp has already returned a response to the browser. This usually results in an exception when the servlet tries to send something else to the browser.

If on the other hand the username corresponds to a user in the user table of the publisher database, the findByUsername method wil return an instance of the user class with the username, pasword and id fields taken from the database. In this case, doPost needs to check that the password submitted by the user matches the password retrieved from the database. We use the equals method of the string class to compare the 2 passwords. If we were to have used the comparison operator == the comparison would be done between the string references rather than the string values. In other words, the comparison would check to see if the 2 string references point to the same object in memory. If the 2 passwords are not equal, doPost returns exactly the same message that it does for the case that the username is not known. It is a security flaw to report to the user that the password is wrong or that the username is wrong, because this enables an attacker to confirm the existence of usernames in the system.

If the 2 passwords match, then the user has successfully authenticated to the system. In this case, we store a value in the session object that indicates the identity of the user. In our case, we will store the id of the user in the session. After doing this, we redirect the user to the home page. Note that we could have forwarded to the home jsp instead of redirecting. However, when forward execution to the jsp, the url displayed to the user will not correspond to the page they are viewing. We can avoid this potential confusion by redirecting the browser to the home page, which means we return an HTTP redirection response to the browser to tell it that it should retrieve content from a different URL.

To understand how attaching the user's identity to the session object works for authentication, you need to understand how the web container creates and uses the session object. The first time the user goes to the web site, the web container returns a set-cookie header along with the HTML comprising the web page. The set-cookie header has a duration attribute set to *session* to let the browser know that the cookie value is to be used to maintain a *session*. A session is a sequence of client-server interactions that can be thought of as comprising a conversion between the client and the server that is distinct from conversions that have taken place in the past or will take place in the future. The set-cookie header contains a long random string of characters that are difficult to guess, so that attackers can not *hijack the session* by pretending to be someone else. The browser caches this cookie for as long as it runs. When the browser shuts down, it generally deletes all its session cookies. Each time the browser sends a reuquest message to the server, it will attach the session cookie value in a cookie header. Therefore, each time the server gets a request, it uses the cookie value to determine which session, or conversion, this request is a part of. The web container provides an instance of the HttpSession class to the web application for each session. Session data is not maintained forever by the server; if a given session cookie is not received by the server after a session time-out value, the server will delete the session data from its memory. Subsequent requests containing that cookie value will result in a new session cookie value sent back to the browser. This is the reason you are logged out of a site automatically after a long period of inactivitiy, even though you did not restart your browser. In Java, the session object is retrieved by calling the getSession method of the request object passed into doGet or doPost. By storing the user's id in the session object, the code running in the application can determine who it is interacting with.

In the jsp folder, create login.jsp with the contents of figure 14.7. In the jsp given above you can see the scriptlet of Java code that pulls out the value associate with the name *message*. If the value is not null, it means the servlet set a message to display. In this case, the jsp writes the message value into the output stream into which the HTML is being written and transported to the browser.

Start and stop the application with the manager application (**http://localhost:8080/manager/html/**) so that Tomcat reprocesses the deployment descriptor and loads new class files. Go to **http://localhost:8080/publisher/login**, type in the username and password of a user and verify that you are sent to the home page. text

Go back to the login page, type in an incorrect username and password, and verify that you are returned to the login page with an error message.

Create a Logout Servlet

So far, we have created a mechanism to log a user in, but we have not yet created a mechanism to log a user out. Recall that a user is logged in when the user's id is stored in the session object. One way to log a person out, therefore, is to delete the id from the session. However, there may be other data stored in the session as well, such as credit card number and other confidential information. It is therefore safer to delete the session altogether. We do this by calling *invalidate* on the session object. The web container will then create a new session object and return a new session cookie to the browser when it receives a log out request.

Add the following lines to the deployment descriptor to configure the logout servlet.

```
<html>
<head>
   <title>Publisher</title>
   <link rel="stylesheet" type="text/css" href="styles.css"/>
</head>
<body>
<h1>Login</h1>
<%
   String message = (String) request.getAttribute("message");
   if (message != null) {
      out.println("<p>" + message + "</p>");
   }
%>

<form method="post" action="">
   <div>
      Username: <input type="text" name="username" size="36" />

   </div>
   <div>
      Password: <input type="password" name="password" size="36" />

   </div>
   <div>
      <input type="submit" value="Login" />
   </div>

</form>
</html>
```

Figure 14.7: login.jsp

```
package publisher.web;

import java.io.IOException;

import javax.servlet.ServletException;
import javax.servlet.http.HttpServlet;
import javax.servlet.http.HttpServletRequest;
import javax.servlet.http.HttpServletResponse;
import javax.servlet.http.HttpSession;

import org.apache.log4j.Logger;

public class LogoutServlet extends HttpServlet
{
    private Logger logger = Logger.getLogger(this.getClass());

    protected void doGet(HttpServletRequest req, HttpServletResponse resp)
    throws ServletException, IOException {
        logger.debug("doGet()");
        HttpSession session = req.getSession();
        session.invalidate();
        String url = "login";
        resp.sendRedirect(url);
    }
}
```

Figure 14.8: class LogoutServlet

```
<servlet>
    <servlet-name>logout</servlet-name>
    <servlet-class>publisher.web.LogoutServlet</servlet-class>
</servlet>

<servlet-mapping>
    <servlet-name>logout</servlet-name>
    <url-pattern>/logout</url-pattern>
</servlet-mapping>
```

Figure 14.8 is the servlet code for the logout servlet. Verify that login/logout function works. Logging in should bring you to the home page; logging out should bring you back to the login page.

At this point, logging in and out has not real effect on the application, because users can access every web page regardless of whether they are logged in or out. In the subsequent section, we will add a filter that filters out requests for web pages that we want to show only to logged in users.

14.6   Security Filter

The purpose of the security filter is to enforce authorization policies for the web application. In other words, the security filter makes sure that users only access the resources for which they are authorized.

A servlet filter is a component that is configured to pre-process and post-process requests that are processed by servlets. By placing security code in a servlet filter, we separate security-related code from code that implements application functionality, which adheres to the separation of concerns principle.

Add the contents of the following code to the deployment descriptor (web.xml).

```
<security-constraint>
   <web-resource-collection>
      <web-resource-name>publisher</web-resource-name>
      <url-pattern>/login</url-pattern>
   </web-resource-collection>
   <user-data-constraint>
      <transport-guarantee>CONFIDENTIAL</transport-guarantee>
   </user-data-constraint>
</security-constraint>

<filter>
   <filter-name>security-filter</filter-name>
   <filter-class>publisher.web.SecurityFilter</filter-class>
</filter>
<filter-mapping>
   <filter-name>security-filter</filter-name>
   <url-pattern>/*</url-pattern>
</filter-mapping>
```

The security-constraint element ensures that access to the login servlet is done over https. (Https is the standard mechanism for providing confidentiality.) The filter element tells the servlet container to pass all requests to the application through the security filter rather than to the target servlet. The security filter then decides whether to pass the request message to the target servlet or redirect the user to the login page.

In the publisher.web package, create a java class called SecurityFilter with the contents of figure 14.9 code.

```
package publisher.web;

import java.io.IOException;

import javax.servlet.Filter;
import javax.servlet.FilterChain;
import javax.servlet.FilterConfig;
import javax.servlet.ServletException;
import javax.servlet.ServletRequest;
import javax.servlet.ServletResponse;
import javax.servlet.http.HttpServletRequest;
import javax.servlet.http.HttpServletResponse;
import javax.servlet.http.HttpSession;

import org.apache.log4j.Logger;

public class SecurityFilter implements Filter
{
    private Logger logger = Logger.getLogger(this.getClass());
    public void init(FilterConfig filterConfig) throws ServletException
    {
    }

    public void destroy()
    {
    }

    public void doFilter(
            ServletRequest request,
            ServletResponse response,
            FilterChain chain)
    throws IOException, ServletException
    {
        logger.debug("doFilter()");
        HttpServletResponse resp = (HttpServletResponse) response;
        HttpServletRequest req = (HttpServletRequest) request;
        String servletPath = req.getServletPath();

        // Allow access to login functionality.
        if (servletPath.equals("/login"))
        {
            chain.doFilter(req, resp);
            return;
        }
        // Allow access to news feed.
```

207

```
      if (servletPath.equals("/news.rss")) {
        chain.doFilter(req, resp);
        return;
      }
      // All other functionality requires authentication.
      HttpSession session = req.getSession();
      Long userId = (Long) session.getAttribute("userId");
      if (userId != null)
      {
          // User is logged in.
          chain.doFilter(req, resp);
          return;
      }

      // Request is not authorized.
      resp.sendRedirect("login");
  }
}
```

Figure 14.9: class SecurityFilter

The init method implemented above does nothing but is needed in the code because the it is a method in the Filter interface. All methods in interfaces must be implemented, so we provide a empty method. Similary, we provide an empty implementation of the destroy method.

The web.xml code given earlier configure this filter to process all requests that come into this application. If the user is not logged in, then we will send the user to the login page. In this way, users can not access any application functionality other than the login page until they authenticate themselves to the system.

The doFilter method of the above filter is called for every requested resource. The first thing we do is check to see if the requested resource is for the login page. Requests for the login page should always be honored, so in this case, we permit the request to be processed by the servlet attached to the incoming request by calling doFilter on the chain object. The chain object represents the chain of processors that will be used for the incoming requests. After calling doFilter on the chain object, we return because at this point, the login servlet would have processed the request.

In addition to login requests, we also want to permit requests for the news feed. This allows anyone to view the news feed. What we want to restrict is access to the functionality that allows users to create, edit and delete news items.

If the request is not for login and not for the news feed, then we need to check to see if the user is logged in. We do this be looking to see if the user's id is stored in the session. If the user's id is in the session, we allow the request to be processed by calling doFilter on the chain object. If the user's id is not in the session, then we redirect the browser to the login page.

Stop and start the publisher application and then perform the following tests with a fresh browser instance.

1. Verify that login and logout functions work correctly.

2. After doing a logout, try to access a protected resource without logging in. For instance, try to access **http://localhost:8080/publisher/home**. Verify that the application redirects you to the login page rather than sending you the home page. If it appears that you can still access a protected resource, then the browser is presenting to you a cached version of the web page. To see that this is the case, click on the reload button of the browser and see that you are redirected to the login page

14.7 Password Digests

If the web application server is compromised (i.e. an attacker has gained access to the server), it is possible for the attacker to get the usernames and passwords from the user table. Even if your application doesn't have highly confidential information, users may have entered passwords that they use to access other applications. To mitigate the potential danger, it is better to store secure digests of user passwords rather than the plaintext (unencrypted) password.

The key property of a secure digest is that it is an irreversible mapping of a string to another string, which means that given the password, you can compute the digest; but given the digest, you can not compute the password. If we store a digest of the passwords in the database, then an attacker who has access to the database can not compute any passwords. If the passwords are simple, the attacker could perform what is referred to as a *dictionary attack* in which he or she tries every password from a list of common or potenital passwords. This threat is mitigated if users choose string passwords.

The web application also can not determine the user passwords from what is stored in the database. However, the password digests are sufficient for authentication. When the user submits a password during authentication, The web application maps the password to its digest and then checks to see if the digest it has just computed matches with the digest stored in the database.

It should be kept in mind that storing digests in the database simply adds a layer of inconvenience to an attacker, and does not provide essential security. If the attacker has access to the database, he or she most likely has access to the the system on which the web application is running. In this case, the attacker can put up an intermediate login page that captures the users' passwords before passing them to the web application. Other attacks are possible as well if the underlying server is not secure or if the web application provides an entry point into the system in some way.

In this section, we add password digesting to the publisher application.

Secure Digester Utility Class

In the publisher.data package, create a class called SecureDigester with the contents figure 14.10. This class can be used to compute secure digests of any string; in our case, we use it to compute the digests of passwsords.

```
package publisher.data;
```

```java
import java.security.MessageDigest;

public class SecureDigester
{
    private static final char digits[] =
    { '0', '1', '2', '3', '4', '5', '6', '7', '8', '9', 'A', 'B', 'C', 'D', 'E',
        'F' };

    private static String byteArrayToHexString(byte[] b)
    {
        StringBuffer hexString = new StringBuffer(b.length);
        for (int i = 0; i < b.length; i++)
        {
            hexString.append(digits[(b[i] & 0xF0) >> 4]);
            hexString.append(digits[b[i] & 0x0F]);
        }
        return hexString.toString();
    }

    public static String digest(String plaintext)
    {
        try
        {
            MessageDigest md = MessageDigest.getInstance("SHA");
            md.update(plaintext.getBytes("UTF-8"));
            byte[] mdBytes = md.digest();
            String hashString = byteArrayToHexString(mdBytes);
            return hashString;
        } catch (Exception e)
        {
            throw new RuntimeException(e);
        }
    }

    public static void main(String args[])
    {
        String password = args[0];
        System.out.println(password + " -> " + digest(password));
    }
}
```

Figure 14.10: class SecureDigester

211

Notice that SecureDigester has a main method. This allows you to run the digester outside the web application for the purpose of generating digests of passwords to include in test data.

The digest function of SecureDigester is the public entry point into the class that will be called by the login servlet to computer password digests. As you can see from the code, the digest method uses the MessageDigest class that is part of the core Java API. MessageDigest has a factory method called getInstance that takes a string that names the hash function to use. In our case, we specify SHA, which is a commonly used secure hash function. The code passes the plaintext string into the update method of the message digest object as a byte array of UTF-8 character codes. Then, the digest method is invoked on the message digest object in order to compute the SHA digest of the byte array. This returns a byte array, which is then transformed into a string by a call to the locally defined byteArrayToHexString. It is this string that the application uses as its version of the password.

Now, modify the login servlet by replacing the password checking code with the following code. Remember to organize imports to resolve the name SecureDigester.

```
String password = req.getParameter("password");
if (password == null)
{
    logger.debug("authentication failed: no password");
    req.setAttribute("message", "Authentication failed.");
    jsp.forward(req, resp);
    return;
}
String passwordDigest = SecureDigester.digest(password);
if (!user.getPassword().equals(passwordDigest))
{
    logger.debug("authentication failed: bad password");
    req.setAttribute("message", "Authentication failed.");
    jsp.forward(req, resp);
    return;
}
```

At this point, in order to login, we need to replace the passwords in the database with their digests as computed by the secure digester class. To do this, we run the secure digester class as a stand-alone program and pass in the password as a command line argument to the program. To do this inside of Eclipse, we create a *run configuration* that specifies the secure digester class as the entry point of execution and enter the password that we wish to encrypt as a program argument. Form the main mennu, select Run ... Run Configurations. Navigate to the publisher project and secure digester main class if these fields are not already set correctly. Figure 14.11 shows the reult.

Select the arguments tab and enter into the program arguments box the password that you wish to encrypt. Figure 14.12 shows the string *admin* being passed in as the password to digest.

After running the secure digester to encrypt a password, look in the console view to see the result. If you entered the string *admin*, the program would generate the following output in the console view.

```
admin -> D033E22AE348AEB5660FC2140AEC35850C4DA997
```

Open the insert_data.sql script and replace the password value of the user with the hex string produced by the secure digester and run the database build file to re-build the database.

Restart the publisher application and verify that the application works correctly.

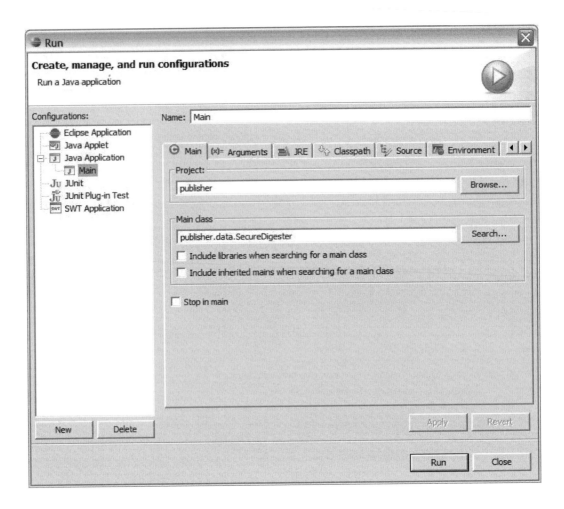

Figure 14.11: Run Window

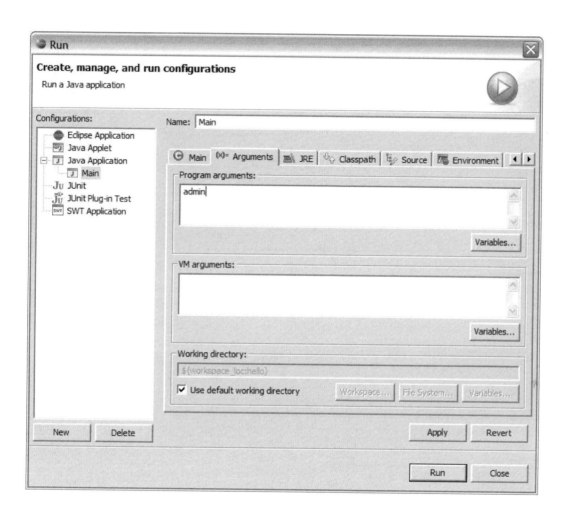

Figure 14.12: ArgumentsTabOfRunWindow

14.8 Exercises

(1) Persistent Sessions :

By default, Tomcat caches sessions between restarts. This means that logged in users will remain logged in after restarting Tomcat. Construct and carry out an experiment to verify this. Study the Tomcat documentation to find out whether session caching can be turned off or whether session caching is always present. If it can be turned off, construct and carry out an experiment to verify this.

(2) Class Hierarchy :

Notice that User and NewsItem both contain an id member variable. Define a new class called PersistentObject that contains a single member variable called id of type long and with protected access. Create getter and setter methods for this member variable. Remove id from User and NewsItem, and have these two classes extend PersistentObject. Test that your application functions correctly with this change.

(3) Elimination of Redundant Code :

Study the classes UserDAO and NewsItemDAO for the presence of redundant code. Devise a means to move this redundancy into their parent class DataAccessObject. Implement and test your design.

(4) User Account Management :

Add user account management functionality to the publisher application that allows the user with username *admin* to list, view, create, edit and delete user accounts. Follow the architecture presented in the chapter on item management. Modify the security filter to only permit only the admin user to access this new functionality.

Chapter 15

Wiki Application Development

15.1 Objectives

- Learn about implementation details behind wiki applications

- Learn how to use stubs to postpone implementation details

- Learn how to use natural primary keys rather than surrogate primary keys

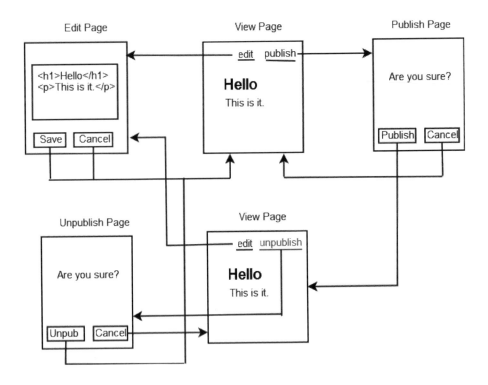

Figure 15.1: Page Flow Diagram For Wiki Application

15.2 Overview

A wiki is a web application that allows users to create and modify web pages. A wiki provides a simple markup language (method of annotating text) that users can use to provide links to other wiki pages and to accomplish simple formatting. In this chapter, we will construct a new web application that implements a simple wiki. To make the implementation simpler, users will use HTML rather than traditional wiki markup when editing page contents. Figure 15.1 illustrates the page flow for the wiki application.

Conceptually, a wiki contains every possible page, which means that all requests for pages are considered valid. If the user requests a page that has never had content added to it, then the user sees a blank page. In the database, only pages that have non-empty content are stored. A page with only white space is considered empty, and is thus not stored in the database. If a user wishes to delete a page, he or she sets its

218

contents to empty, and the application will then delete the page from the database.

Note that in wiki systems such as the open source project used by Wikipedia, called MediaWiki, the history of edits to pages are saved so that users can restore previously deleted content or simply view previous versions of a page. In our simple wiki, we will not store previous versions of pages, which could be a great inconvenience in a real usage scenario.

In our wiki system, users see an edit link and a publish link on each page. To change the contents of the page, whether it is an initial entry or a mofification to existing content, the users selects the edit link and transitions to an edit page. In the edit page, the user can modify the contents of the page and then either save or cancel changes. In both cases, the user is brought back to the view page.

The above diagram actually shows two versions of the view page: one with a publish link and one with an unpublish link. In this wiki system, we will be able to create and delete news feed entries in the publisher application that refer to wiki pages. If a given wiki page is not registered with the publisher application, then the publish link is shown. If the user clicks on the publish link, he or she is brought to the publish page, which is a confirmation window. If the user confirms the publish operation, the system returns the view page with the unpublish link to indicate that the page is in the news feed and to give the user the ability to remove the page from the news feed. If the user cancels the publish operation, he or she is brought back to the view page with the publish link.

The unpublish link goes to the unpublish page, which is also a confirmation page.

In this chapter, we will build all the above functionality, however we will implement the publish and unpublish operations as stubs. The term *stub* is used to describe a function that is declared and callable, but has no effect; it is used as a placeholder for the real implementation to be done at a later time.

In the chapter that follows, we implement the publish and unpublish operations as web services in the publisher application. The wiki application will then invoke these web services to create and delete news feed entries for wiki pages.

15.3 Project Creation

In this section, you will build the database needed for the wiki application. However, before starting on this task, you need to first create a new Eclipse project that will hold the database scripts and the other source code that you will build in subsequent sections of this chapter.

In Eclipse, create a new project called wiki using a procedure similar to the one you used to create the website and publisher projects. Pay particular attention to configuring logging. You will be creating java classes with package names that start with wiki. In order that debug-level log messages are written into the log file, the last line in the log4j.properties file should include a reference to wiki rather than publisher, as given in the following line

```
log4j.logger.wiki=DEBUG
```

Database Creation

In this section, you will create a database for the wiki application and set up an ant build file to run database scripts that drop tables, create tables and insert test data. Recall that with these database scripts, it is easy to modify the database as your web application evolves.

Use the MySQL command line client to create a database with name wiki. The following two commands show how to do this.

```
mysql> create database wiki;
mysql> grant all privileges on wiki.* to 'wiki'@'localhost' identified by '1234';
```

Similar to the publisher project, you should create a folder called database to store database creation scripts and the ant build file to run them. To begin, copy the database folder in the publisher project into the wiki project. In the subsequent steps, we will modify these copied files to work correctly for the wiki application.

In the database folder, modify build.xml so that you operate on the wiki database rather than the publisher database. To do this, you only need to modify the property element that sets the value of the *mysql.params* attribute. The property element should appear as follows.

```
create table page
(
    name varchar(255) primary key,
    content text not null,
    published int default 0,
    published_id varchar(255)
);
```

Figure 15.2: createdb.sql

```
<property name="mysql.params" value="-u wiki -p1234 -D wiki" />
```

Replace the contents of createdb.sql with the contents of figure 15.2.

The name column will hold the name of the wiki page. We use the wiki page name as the primary key rather than using a separate integer id as we did in the publisher application. Using page name as primary key works, because page names need to be unique, which is the main requirement for data to serve as a primary key. The name column has datatype varchar(255), which means that this column will hold variable lengths character strings that can not exceed a length of 255. Varchar columns can be used as primary keys. The content column will contain the character data that comprises the wiki pages; it has datatype text, which allows for the storage of a large number of characters. Text columns can not be used as primary keys. The published column is an integer that will hold a zero or a one, where zero indicates that the page has not been added to the publisher application and one indicates that it has. The published column defaults to 0, meaning that if a value for this column is not specified when a new row is inserted into the wiki page table, then the published column will default to 0. The published_id column holds the id of the news item in the publisher application that references the wiki page represented by this row. If a given page is not published, the state of the published_id column has no meaning to the application.

Modify insertdb.sql, so that you create at least two sample pages. You only need to specify values for the name and content columns because the published column defaults to 0, which represents false, and the value of published_id will not be used when published is false. You should create a row to represent the page whose name is the empty string, because this will be the page with no name and can serve as the start page in the wiki system. Use the contents of figure 15.3 for insert_data.sql.

```
insert into page (name, content) values ('', '<h1>Nameless Page</h1>
<a href="hello">hello page</a><br /><a href="nowhere">nowhere page</a>');

insert into page (name, content) values ('hello', '<h1>Hello Page</h1>
<a href=".">nameless page</a>');
```

Figure 15.3: insertdb.sql

Notice that in the above 2 insert statements we store HTML content directly in the database. Normally in a wiki application users do not enter HTML directly into the application. Instead, they enter character data that is annotated with wiki markup conventions. An example of *wiki markup* is to use apostrophes to italicize words.

The first of the above insert statements creates a page with name equal to the empty string. We refer to this page as the nameless page, or the root page. Insde the nameless page there are 2 links. The first link goes to a page with name *hello*, which is a nonempty page created by the second insert command. The second link in the nameless page goes to a page called nowhere, which does not exist in the database. When the user follows the link to the nowhere page, he or she will see a blank page that can be modified.

Finally, modify cleandb.sql with the contents of the following listing.

cleandb.sql

```
drop table if exists page;
```

The above statement is not generic SQL syntax. The `if exists [page]` part of the statement is supported by MySQL, but is not necessarily support by other database systems. This MySQL extension to the SQL definition is convenient because one can issue a drop table command for a table that may not exist. Using this exension, however, breaks the portability of our application. If we want to use another database system, we would most likely need to modify this script.

Run the *all* target of the build file to create and populate the page table of the wiki database.

15.4 Persistence Classes

Overview

In this section, you will create the classes that store and manage the persistent data of the application. Specifically, a page class and its corresponding DAO will be defined. In preparation for adding additional persistent classes, we create a parent DAO that the page DAO extends. Data access object classes for other persistent classes can then be added more easily by subclassing the parent DAO.

There is one important difference between the persistence system in the wiki application and the publisher application: the wiki application will use natural primary keys as opposed to surrogate primary keys used in the publsiher application. This is done for two reasons. First, by using the page name for primary key, we avoid the extra complexity of generating unique integers. Second, it allows us as students to learn about the two different approaches and how to carry these out in Java web applications.

Setup Logging

Before defining any classes, we should set up the application for logging. Similar to the other application projects, create a lib folder under *web/WEB-INF* and place the log4j jar file into it. This adds adds log4j to the runtime classpath that the class loader for the web application will search. Additionally, you need to add the log4j jar file to the build path so that the compiler can load log4j class definitions.

Also similar to the other applications, create log4j.properties in the src folder, and add configuration similar to that used in the publisher and website applications.

Page Class

We define a page class in package *wiki.data* that contains as member variables the column data stored in the database. The class has the following attributes.

```
private String name;
private String content;
private boolean published;
private String publishedId;
```

The page class is simply a container of information; it contains no logic other than that needed to provide access to its data members. Instance of classes such as the page class are sometimes referred to as value objects because that simply represent data without behavior. The complete listing of the page class is in figure 15.4.

We could have avoided implementing the accessor methods (getters and setters) in the page class by simply declaring the member variables public. However, this is a bad idea for 2 reasons. First, making member variables private is a common coding convention (called the JavaBean convention) followed by the majority of Java programmers, so deviating from the convention makes the code less readable by a wider audience. Second, the choice of accessor name is necessary in order to use the JSP expression language. For example, suppose you are in a jsp file and have a variable called wikiPage that contains a reference to an instance of a wiki page. To write the name of the wiki page into the outgoing stream of HTML, you could simply use the following expression.

```
${wikiPage.name}
```

The expression language processes the above expression by capitalizing the n in name to become Name and then it prepends get to this, resulting in the string *getName*. The expression language then uses this string to get an instance of the getName method of the page class. The ability is provided by what is referred to as the *reflection API*, which is available in *managed execution environments* in which virtual machine code runs inside a virtual machine. Systems other than the JSP expression language, such as Hibernate for example, rely on the JavaBean convention for naming getter and setter methods. Thus to avoid interoperability problems with other systems, one should adhere to the convention.

Note that the above exmaple is not really shorter than what is possible without the expression language. For example, the following scriplet is equivalent to the above example.

```
<%= wikiPage.getName() %>
```

Data Access Object Super Class

Similar to the publisher application, we avoid duplication of code in the data access object classes by placing common functionality into a parent class called *DataAccessObject*. Figure 15.5 shows the contents of this class.

```
package wiki.data;

public class Page {
        private String name;
        private String content;
        private boolean published;
        private String publishedId;

        public String getContent() {
                return content;
        }

        public void setContent(String content) {
                this.content = content;
        }

        public String getName() {
                return name;
        }

        public void setName(String name) {
                this.name = name;
        }

        public boolean isPublished() {
                return published;
        }

        public void setPublished(boolean published) {
                this.published = published;
        }

        public String getPublishedId() {
                return publishedId;
        }

        public void setPublishedId(String publishedId) {
                this.publishedId = publishedId;
        }
}
```

Figure 15.4: Page.java

225

```
DataAccessObject.java
package wiki.data;

import java.sql.Connection;
import java.sql.ResultSet;
import java.sql.SQLException;
import java.sql.Statement;

import javax.sql.DataSource;

public class DataAccessObject {
    private static DataSource dataSource;

    public static void setDataSource(DataSource dataSource)
    {
        DataAccessObject.dataSource = dataSource;
    }

    protected static Connection getConnection()
    {
        try {
            return dataSource.getConnection();
        } catch (SQLException e) {
            throw new RuntimeException(e);
        }
    }

    protected static void close(Statement statement, Connection connection)
    {
        close(null, statement, connection);
    }

    protected static void close(ResultSet rs, Statement statement,
            Connection connection)
    {
        try {
            if (rs != null)
                rs.close();
            if (statement != null)
                statement.close();
            if (connection != null)
                connection.close();
        } catch (SQLException e) {
            throw new RuntimeException(e);
        }
```

```
    }
}
```

Figure 15.5: class DataAccessObject

The data access object parent class is simpler than the one used for the publisher application because it does not to include code that generates unique integers for use as primary keys.

The Page DAO Class

Figure 15.6 shows the contents of the page DAO.

```
package wiki.data;

import java.sql.Connection;
import java.sql.PreparedStatement;
import java.sql.ResultSet;
import java.sql.SQLException;

public class PageDAO extends DataAccessObject {

        private static PageDAO instance = new PageDAO();

        public static PageDAO getInstance() {
                return instance;
        }

        private Page read(ResultSet rs) throws SQLException {
                String name = rs.getString("name");
                String content = rs.getString("content");
                boolean published = rs.getBoolean("published");
                String publishedId = rs.getString("published_id");
                Page page = new Page();
                page.setName(name);
                page.setContent(content);
                page.setPublished(published);
                page.setPublishedId(publishedId);
                return page;
        }
```

```java
public Page find(String name) {
        ResultSet rs = null;
        PreparedStatement statement = null;
        Connection connection = null;
        try {
                connection = getConnection();
                String sql = "select * from page where name=?";
                statement = connection.prepareStatement(sql);
                statement.setString(1, name);
                rs = statement.executeQuery();
                if (!rs.next()) {
                        return null;
                }
                return read(rs);
        } catch (SQLException e) {
                throw new RuntimeException(e);
        } finally {
                close(rs, statement, connection);
        }
}

public void update(Page page) {
        PreparedStatement statement = null;
        Connection connection = null;
        try {
                connection = getConnection();
                String sql = "update page set content=?, published=?,
    published_id=? where name=?";
                statement = connection.prepareStatement(sql);
                statement.setString(1, page.getContent());
                statement.setBoolean(2, page.isPublished());
                statement.setString(3, page.getPublishedId());
                statement.setString(4, page.getName());
                statement.executeUpdate();
        } catch (SQLException e) {
                throw new RuntimeException(e);
        } finally {
                close(statement, connection);
        }
}

public void create(Page page) {
        PreparedStatement statement = null;
        Connection connection = null;
        try {
```

228

```
                connection = getConnection();
                String sql = "insert into page (name, content) values (?, ?)";
                statement = connection.prepareStatement(sql);
                statement.setString(1, page.getName());
                statement.setString(2, page.getContent());
                statement.executeUpdate();
        } catch (SQLException e) {
                throw new RuntimeException(e);
        } finally {
                close(statement, connection);
        }
    }

    public void delete(Page page) {
            PreparedStatement statement = null;
            Connection connection = null;
            try {
                    connection = getConnection();
                    String sql = "delete from page where name=?";
                    statement = connection.prepareStatement(sql);
                    String name = page.getName();
                    statement.setString(1, name);
                    statement.executeUpdate();
            } catch (SQLException e) {
                    throw new RuntimeException(e);
            } finally {
                    close(statement, connection);
            }
    }
}
```

Figure 15.6: class PageDAO

The Init Class

We add figure 15.7 implementation of the init class in order to establish a reference to the data source that we will configure through the context element. We place this class in the wiki.web package because it is an initialization class that is configured into Tomcat. It could be reasonably argued that this could be alternatively located in the wiki.data package.

```
package wiki.web;

import javax.naming.Context;
import javax.naming.InitialContext;
import javax.servlet.ServletContext;
import javax.servlet.ServletContextEvent;
import javax.servlet.ServletContextListener;
import javax.sql.DataSource;

import org.apache.log4j.Logger;

import wiki.data.DataAccessObject;

public class Init implements ServletContextListener {

    private Logger logger = Logger.getLogger(this.getClass());

    public void contextDestroyed(ServletContextEvent sce) {
    }

    private void contextInitialized2(ServletContext servletContext)
    throws Exception {
        InitialContext enc = new InitialContext();
        Context compContext = (Context) enc.lookup("java:comp/env");
        DataSource dataSource = (DataSource) compContext.lookup("datasource");
        DataAccessObject.setDataSource(dataSource);
    }

    public void contextInitialized(ServletContextEvent sce) {
        ServletContext servletContext = sce.getServletContext();
        try {
            contextInitialized2(servletContext);
        }
        catch (Exception e)
        {
            logger.error("Initialization failed.", e);
            throw new RuntimeException(e);
        }
        logger.debug("Initialization succeeded.");
    }
}
```

If you have build errors, make sure that you have included servlet_api.jar in the project build path

Figure 15.7: class Init

15.5　View Page

Overview

In this section we create and configure the servlet and jsp needed to let users view wiki pages.

JSP

Within the web/WEB-INF folder, create a new folder called jsp. Within the jsp folder create a file called view-page.jsp with the contents of figure 15.8.

```
<jsp:useBean id="wikipage" scope="request" type="wiki.data.Page" />
<html>
<head>
    <title>Wiki</title>
    <link rel="stylesheet" type="text/css" href="../styles.css" />
</head>
<body>

<table border="0" cellspacing="0" cellpadding="0">
    <tr>
        <td><img src="../images/logo.gif"></td>
    </tr>
    <tr>
        <td id="upper-bar">
            <div id="upper-menu">
                <a href="../edit/${wikipage.name}">edit</a>
                |
                <%
                    if (wikipage.isPublished()) {
                %>
                <a href="../unpublish/${wikipage.name}">unpublish</a>
                <%
                    } else {
                %>
                <a href="../publish/${wikipage.name}">publish</a>
                <%
                    }
                %>
            </div>
        </td>
    </tr>
    <tr>
```

```
<td id="lower-bar">
    <div id="layout">
        ${wikipage.content}
    </div>
</td>
</tr>
</table>

</body>
</html>
```

Figure 15.8: view-page.jsp

Observe that the page is parameterized by a single variable, wikipage. Before forwarding to this JSP, the servlet constructs the *wikipage* instance and places it in request scope by associating the name wikipage with an instance of the *page* class. We avoid using the name page for this purpose because this is a reserved identifier used by JSP to reference something called the JSP page object.

The view page uses a table to organize the layout of the page. After the useBean element at the top of the JSP, the next instance of dynamic content is the construction of an edit link. In this edit link, we add the name of the wiki page that we are viewing. When the user clicks the link to edit the page, the browser sends a request with the string *edit/* followed by the wiki page name.

After constructing the edit link, the JSP file contains a conditional expression that test whether or not the page is published in the publisher application. If the page is published, then the JSP generates a link that goes to the unpublish servlet. If the page is not published, the JSP generates a link that goes to the publish servlet. These two servlets will be constructed in a later section.

The last piece of dynamic content to appear in the view jsp file is the page content.

Notice that the image tag refers to a logo file in the images folder. This logo will be displayed as the page banner. You should create this folder and place a logo file in there.

Also notice that the JSP contains in the HTML head section a reference to a style sheet. You should create this file in the web folder with figure 15.9.

The View Page Servlet

Add the view page servlet to the project with figure 15.10 implementation.

```
h1 {
   color: #000088;
}

#layout {
      margin: 1em;
}

#upper-menu {
      margin: 0.5em;
      text-align: right;
}

#upper-bar {
      background-color: #E6E6FA;
}

#lower-bar {
      background-color: #F5F5DC;
}
```

Figure 15.9: styles.css

```
package wiki.web;

import java.io.IOException;

import javax.servlet.RequestDispatcher;
import javax.servlet.ServletConfig;
import javax.servlet.ServletContext;
import javax.servlet.ServletException;
import javax.servlet.http.HttpServlet;
import javax.servlet.http.HttpServletRequest;
import javax.servlet.http.HttpServletResponse;

import org.apache.log4j.Logger;

import wiki.data.Page;
import wiki.data.PageDAO;

public class ViewPageServlet extends HttpServlet {

        private Logger logger = Logger.getLogger(this.getClass());
        private RequestDispatcher jsp;

        public void init(ServletConfig config) throws ServletException {
                ServletContext context = config.getServletContext();
                jsp = context.getRequestDispatcher("/WEB-INF/jsp/view-page.jsp");
        }

        protected void doGet(HttpServletRequest req, HttpServletResponse resp)
                        throws ServletException, IOException {
                logger.debug("doGet()");
                String pathInfo = req.getPathInfo();
                String name = pathInfo.substring(1);
                logger.debug("Page requested: " + name);
                Page page = new PageDAO().find(name);
                if (page == null) {
                        logger.debug("page doesn't exist; creating empty page");
                        page = new Page();
                        page.setName(name);
                        page.setContent("");
                        page.setPublished(false);
                }
                req.setAttribute("wikipage", page);
                jsp.forward(req, resp);
```

```
        }
}
```

Figure 15.10: ViewPageServlet.java

In a manner similar to the servlets in the publisher application, we override the init(ServletConfig) method in order to set the value of the request dispatcher that we will use to forward execution to the JSP.

The first thing we do after writing a log message is to determine the page name being requested by the user. We call getPathInfo on the request object to get the string within the url that follows /view. Because this string begins with a slash, we remove the slash with the substring method. This leaves the name of the wiki page. We print the page name in the log file, and then we use the name to retrieve the page object from the database.

If the page is not in the database, the page DAO will return null. In this case, we create a new page instance, set its name property to the page name being requested. We also set the page content to the empty string and the publsihed attribute to false.

After we have either retrieved an existing page or creted a new empty one, we put the page object in request scope by associating it with the name *wikipage*. The JSP will now be able to access the information it needs from this page object.

Add figure 15.11 deployment descriptor (web.xml) to the wiki application.

Deploy

Deploy the wiki application to the path /wiki in a manner similar to how you deployed the publisher application. The context element will look like figure 15.12. Make sure you replace ${WORKSPACE} with the path to your eclipse workspace. Additionally, make sure the database parameters are correct.

If you are not sure that you deployed the application correctly, then check to see that deployment succeeded by looking in ${TOMCAT}/conf/Catalina/localhost. You should see the file *wiki.xml*. Open this file and verify that it is identical to the wiki.xml given above that you placed in your wiki project folder.

If deployment succeeded, but the application is still not working correctly, then look in all the log files for messages. If there is an error related to connecting to the database, make sure that all the arguments in the context element in wiki.xml are correct.

```
<?xml version="1.0"?>
<web-app
xmlns="http://java.sun.com/xml/ns/j2ee"
xmlns:xsi="http://www.w3.org/2001/XMLSchema-instance"
xsi:schemaLocation="http://java.sun.com/xml/ns/j2ee
http://java.sun.com/xml/ns/j2ee/web-app_2_4.xsd"
version="2.4">
    <listener>
        <listener-class>wiki.web.Init</listener-class>
    </listener>
    <servlet>
        <servlet-name>view-page</servlet-name>
        <servlet-class>wiki.web.ViewPageServlet</servlet-class>
    </servlet>
    <servlet-mapping>
        <servlet-name>view-page</servlet-name>
        <url-pattern>/view/*</url-pattern>
    </servlet-mapping>
</web-app>
```

Figure 15.11: The Deployment Descriptor

```
<Context path="/wiki" docBase="${WORKSPACE}\wiki\web">
    <Resource name="datasource"
              type="javax.sql.DataSource"
              auth="Container"
              maxActive="10"
              maxIdle="3"
              maxWait="10000"
              username="wiki"
              password="1234"
              driverClassName="com.mysql.jdbc.Driver"
              url="jdbc:mysql://localhost:3306/wiki?autoReconnect=true" />
</Context>
```

Figure 15.12: wiki context element

237

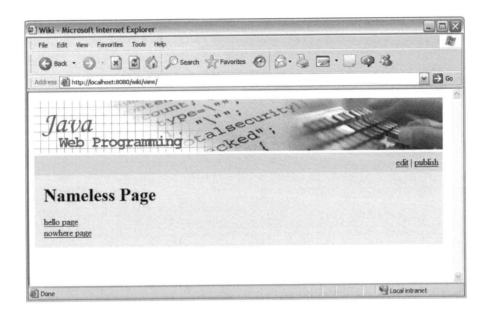

Figure 15.13: View Page

Test

Go to **http://localhost:8080/wiki/view/** to view the page with no name as shown in Figure 15.13. Click on the hello link and see that you go to the hello page. Click on the nowhere link and see that an empty page is generated.

```
<jsp:useBean id="wikipage" scope="request" type="wiki.data.Page" />

<html>
<head>
   <title>Wiki</title>
   <link rel="stylesheet" type="text/css" href="../styles.css" />

</head>
<body>

<form method="post">
   <input type="submit" name="save-button" value="Save" />

   <input type="submit" name="cancel-button" value="Cancel" />
   <input type="hidden" name="name" value="${wikipage.name}" />

   <input type="hidden" name="published" value="${wikipage.published}" />
   <br />
   <textarea name="content" cols="50" rows="15">${wikipage.content}</textarea>

</form>

</body>
</html>
```

Figure 15.14: edit-page.jsp

15.6   Edit Page

Overview

In this section you will create and configure the servlet and jsp needed to let users edit wiki pages.

The JSP

Create *edit-page.jsp* in the jsp folder with the contents of figure 15.14.

The first line tells the JSP translator to generate code that retrieves the value of a page obejct that has been associated with the key *wikipage* in the request object. The form element does not contain an action method, so the browser will submit form data to the same URL that it used to retrieve the form data. The first two input

239

elements in the form are save and cancel buttons. The save button has the attribute name set to save-button and the cancel button has the attribute name set to *cancel-button*. When the edit page servlet receives a submission from the browser, it will check for the presence of a parameter that has name save-button or cancel-button, and will thus be able to determine which button the user clicked.

The third input element is a hidden element with the page name set as the value of *name*. Browsers do not display hidden input elements to the user. Hidden input elements are used to carry information that is sent to the server with the rest of the form data. In this case, the hidden element is used to send the name of the page to the edit servlet. This is neccessary because the edit servlet needs to know which page is being updated.

The forth element is also a hidden element. It is used to carry the state of the published attribute. This information is actually not needed at this point, because once the edit servlet has the page name, it can determine the state of the published attribute.

The final input control within the form is a *textarea* element. This element displays as a multi-line editable text box. The current contents of the given page will be displayed in this text area.

The Edit Page Servlet

The following listing shows the contents of EditPageServlet.java.

```
package wiki.web;

import java.io.IOException;

import javax.servlet.RequestDispatcher;
import javax.servlet.ServletConfig;
import javax.servlet.ServletContext;
import javax.servlet.ServletException;
import javax.servlet.http.HttpServlet;
import javax.servlet.http.HttpServletRequest;
import javax.servlet.http.HttpServletResponse;

import org.apache.log4j.Logger;

import wiki.data.Page;
```

240

```
import wiki.data.PageDAO;

public class EditPageServlet extends HttpServlet {
        private Logger logger = Logger.getLogger(this.getClass());

        private RequestDispatcher jsp;

        public void init(ServletConfig config) throws ServletException {
                ServletContext context = config.getServletContext();
                jsp = context.getRequestDispatcher("/WEB-INF/jsp/edit-page.jsp");
        }

        protected void doGet(HttpServletRequest req, HttpServletResponse resp)
                        throws ServletException, IOException {
                logger.debug("doGet()");
                String pathInfo = req.getPathInfo();
                String name = pathInfo.substring(1);
                logger.debug("Page requested: " + name);
                Page page = new PageDAO().find(name);
                if (page == null) {
                        logger.debug("page doesn't exist; creating empty page");
                        page = new Page();
                        page.setName(name);
                        page.setContent("");
                        page.setPublished(false);
                }
                req.setAttribute("wikipage", page);
                jsp.forward(req, resp);
        }

        protected void doPost(HttpServletRequest req, HttpServletResponse resp)
                        throws ServletException, IOException {
                logger.debug("doPost()");

                // Extract form data.
                String pageName = req.getParameter("name");
                String content = req.getParameter("content");
                String publishedString = req.getParameter("published");
                Boolean publishedBoolean = Boolean.valueOf(publishedString);
                boolean published = publishedBoolean.booleanValue();

                // Check for cancel button.
                String cancelButton = req.getParameter("cancel-button");
                if (cancelButton != null) {
                        resp.sendRedirect("../view/" + pageName);
```

241

```
                        return;
        }

        // Prepare a page object.
        PageDAO pageDAO = new PageDAO();
        Page page = new Page();
        page.setName(pageName);
        page.setContent(content);
        page.setPublished(published);

        // Check to see if user is setting page content to nothing (or all
        // spaces).
        if (content.trim().length() == 0) {
                pageDAO.delete(page);
                resp.sendRedirect("../view/" + page.getName());
                return;
        }

        // Create or update page as appropriate.
        if (pageDAO.find(pageName) == null) {
                // Page doesn't exist; insert into database.
                pageDAO.create(page);
        } else {
                // Page exists; update database.
                pageDAO.update(page);
        }
        resp.sendRedirect("../view/" + page.getName());
    }
}
```

Figure 15.15: EditPageServlet.java

The doGet method of the edit page servlet is identical to the view page servlet. In both servlets, the doGet method must retrieve or create a wiki page object and pass this to its JSP. In the case of the view page servlet, the JSP displays the contents of the wiki page within a div element. In the case of the edit page servlet, the JSP places the contents of the page in an editable text area within a form element. So although the two different JSPs use the wiki page object in different ways, they both need the same object.

The view page and edit page servlets differ in that the edit page servlet implements a doPost method, which the view page servlet does not have. The doPost method of the edit page servlet receives form data from the browser when the user submits changes to the page contents. The first thing the doPost method does is extract references to the form data and stores them in variables.

After extracting the form data, the doPost method checks to see if the cancel button was clicked, in which case the user does not want to save changes to the page. In this case, we return an HTTP redirect message to the browser telling it to request the view page for the page that was in the edit window. We return after sending this message to the browser, because no other work is needed.

If on the other hand the user is not canceling the edit, we need to store changes to the page in the database. We do this by constructing a new page object with the data submitted by the user. If the user is submitting an empty string, or a string of blank characters, then we delete the page from the database. We do this by calling the delete method of the page DAO. Note that we do not need to check to see whether or not the page exists in the database because if the page does not exist, the SQL delete command will have no effect and will not throw an exception.

If the user is submitting non-empty page content, then we need to check to see whether or not the page exists. If the page does not exist, we call the create method of the page DAO, passing in the new page to create. If the page exists, then we call the update method of the page DAO. The create method uses an SQL insert command and the update method uses an SQL update command.

It is possible for one user to delete a page from the database just before another user saves changes to the page. In this case, the update method of the page DAO will throw an exception because it submitted an update command for a row that doesn't exist. Further work would need to be done with the wiki application to handle this problem without displaying an exception to the end user.

Modify Deployment Descriptor

The following XML fragment needs to be added to the deployment descriptor to configure the edit page servlet.

```
<servlet>
    <servlet-name>edit-page</servlet-name>
    <servlet-class>wiki.web.EditPageServlet</servlet-class>
</servlet>
<servlet-mapping>
    <servlet-name>edit-page</servlet-name>
    <url-pattern>/edit/*</url-pattern>
</servlet-mapping>
```

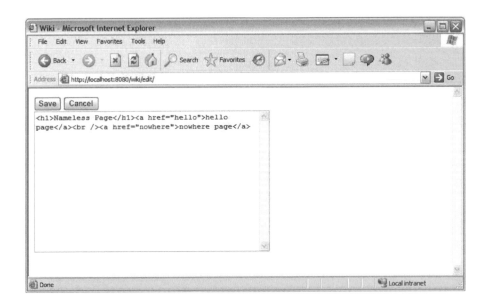

Figure 15.16: Edit Page

Note that the url pattern is similar to the one used to direct requests to the view page servlet. Although other approaches are possible, we use this one in order to match with the way we route to the view servlet.

Test

Stop and start the wiki application with the manager application(**http://localhost:8080/manager/html/**). Then test the new functionality by going to **http://localhost:8080/wiki/view/** and trying to edit the page. The edit page should look like Figure 15.16. text

244

```
<jsp:useBean id="wikipage" scope="request" type="wiki.data.Page" />

<p>
Are you sure you want to publish this page?
</p>

<form method="post">
   <input type="submit" name="publish-button" value="Publish" />
   <input type="submit" name="cancel-button" value="Cancel" />
   <input type="hidden" name="name" value="${wikipage.name}" />
</form>
```

Figure 15.17: publish-page.jsp

15.7   Publish Page

Overview

In this section, we create and configure the servlet and jsp needed to let users publish wiki pages to the publisher application. However, we will not actually make a connection to the publisher application until the next chapter. Therefore, the partial implementation that we provide will serve as a placeholder for the complete solution to be implemented in the next chapter after adding a programmatic interface, called a web service, to the publisher application that allows the wiki application to add and remove news items to its news feed.

The JSP

Figure 15.17 contains the contents of the JSP file that will be used to confirm that the user wishes to publish a given wiki page.

The Publish Page Servlet

The implementation of the publish page servlet is shown in Figure 15.18.

PublishPageServlet.java

```
package wiki.web;
```

245

```java
import java.io.IOException;

import javax.servlet.RequestDispatcher;
import javax.servlet.ServletConfig;
import javax.servlet.ServletContext;
import javax.servlet.ServletException;
import javax.servlet.http.HttpServlet;
import javax.servlet.http.HttpServletRequest;
import javax.servlet.http.HttpServletResponse;

import org.apache.log4j.Logger;

import wiki.data.Page;
import wiki.data.PageDAO;

public class PublishPageServlet extends HttpServlet {
        private Logger logger = Logger.getLogger(this.getClass());

        private RequestDispatcher jsp;

        public void init(ServletConfig config) throws ServletException {
                ServletContext context = config.getServletContext();
                jsp = context.getRequestDispatcher("/WEB-INF/jsp/publish-page.jsp");
        }

        protected void doGet(HttpServletRequest req, HttpServletResponse resp)
                        throws ServletException, IOException {
                logger.debug("doGet()");
                String pathInfo = req.getPathInfo();
                String name = pathInfo.substring(1);
                logger.debug("Page requested: " + name);
                Page page = new PageDAO().find(name);
                if (page == null) {
                        logger.debug("page doesn't exist; creating empty page");
                        page = new Page();
                        page.setName(name);
                        page.setContent("");
                        page.setPublished(false);
                }
                req.setAttribute("wikipage", page);
                jsp.forward(req, resp);
        }

        protected void doPost(HttpServletRequest req, HttpServletResponse resp)
                        throws ServletException, IOException {
```

```
logger.debug("doPost()");

// extract form data
String pageName = req.getParameter("name");

// Check for cancel button.
String cancelButton = req.getParameter("cancel-button");
if (cancelButton != null)
{
    resp.sendRedirect("../view/" + pageName);
    return;
}

PageDAO pageDAO = new PageDAO();
Page page = pageDAO.find(pageName);

// Don't do anything if page doesn't exist or is already published.
if (page == null || page.isPublished())
{
    resp.sendRedirect("../view/" + pageName);
    return;
}

// Invoke remote web service to publish page.
logger.debug("invoking web service");
try
{
    String publishedId = publish(page);
    page.setPublishedId(publishedId);
    page.setPublished(true);
}
catch (Exception e)
{
    logger.error(e);
    throw new RuntimeException(e);
}

// Update page.
pageDAO.update(page);

resp.sendRedirect("../view/" + page.getName());
}

private String publish(Page page) throws IOException
{
```

247

```
            return "3";  // Pretend that publish service returned an id of 3.
    }
}
```

Figure 15.18: PublishPageServlet.java

The doGet method of the publish page servlet is requested by the browser when the user clicks on the publish link that appears within the view page. The doGet method as implemented above allows empty pages to be published. For this reason, the method must create an instance of the wiki page class if the find method of the page DAO returns null. The doGet method forwards execution to the publish page JSP, which asks the user to confirm the operation.

In the publish page JSP, the user either clicks the publish button or the cancel button. Regardless of whether the publish or cancel buttons are clicked, the doPost method needs to know which page the user is on. If he or she clicks the cancel button, the doPost method redirects the the user back to the view page. The user can verify that the page is not published by seeing that the publish option is still available for the page.

If the user is confirming the publish operation, the next thing we do is to retrieve an instance of the page from the database. If the page does not exist in the database, it mean the user is publishing an empty page. We do not allow publishing of blank pages, so we redirect the user to the view page. However, the user will see the publish link in the view page, which may implies that page is not published. Additionally, if the page is already published, we do the same thing.

If the page exists in the database, then we invoke the publish web service of the publisher application, which will be implemented in the next chapter. We place all of the logic for this web service invocation in a private method called *publish*. When we invoke the publish service, we will obtain a news feed id as a result. To prepare for this evetuality, we create a news feed id, called publishedId, and set it to the artificial value 3 for testing purposes. Note that we declare the publish method as throwing an exception to prepare for later code that communicates with the publisher application and thus will be capable of throwing exceptions related to communciation, XML document procesing and other sources of exceptions.

After invoking the publish web service, we need to save the published id with the rest of the page data and we need to set the isPublished property of the wiki page to true. After doing this, we redirect the user to the view page, where he can now see

248

the unpublished link, which is implicit confirmation of the publish operation.

Modify Deployment Descriptor

The following XML fragment needs to be added to the deployment descriptor to configure the publish servlet.

```xml
<servlet>
   <servlet-name>publish-page</servlet-name>
   <servlet-class>wiki.web.PublishPageServlet</servlet-class>
</servlet>
<servlet-mapping>
   <servlet-name>publish-page</servlet-name>
   <url-pattern>/publish/*</url-pattern>
</servlet-mapping>
```

Test

Stop and start the wiki application with the manager application(**http://localhost:8080/manager/html/**). Then test the new functionality by going to **http://localhost:8080/wiki/view/** and clicking on the publish link. Verify that the publish confirmation page displays correctly as shown in Figure 15.19.

Try canceling the operation and then verifying that the publish link is displayed in the view page. The try the publish link again but this time confirm the publish operation. Verify that the link turns to unpublished as shown in Figure 15.20.

249

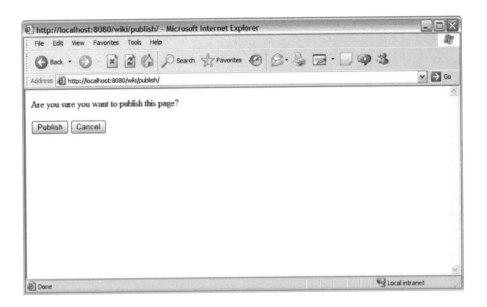

Figure 15.19: Publish Page

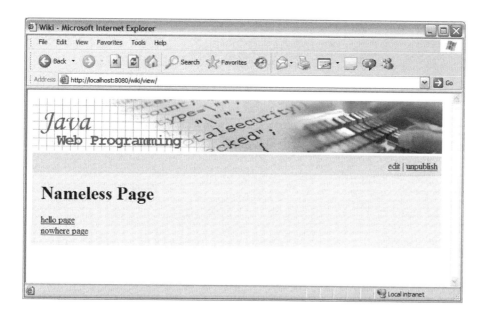

Figure 15.20: Publish Menu Becomes Unpublish

```
<jsp:useBean id="wikipage" scope="request" type="wiki.data.Page" />
<p>
Are you sure you want to unpublish this page?
</p>

<form method="post">
   <input type="submit" name="publish-button" value="Unpublish" />
   <input type="submit" name="cancel-button" value="Cancel" />
   <input type="hidden" name="name" value="${wikipage.name}" />
</form>
```

Figure 15.21: unpublish-page.jsp

15.8 Unpublish Page

Overview

In this section you will create and configure the servlet and jsp needed to let users unpublish wiki pages. However, we will not actually make a connection to the publisher application until the next chapter on web services.

Remember that the publisher application uses 2 different approaches to web service invocation. The publish operation is done through submission of an XML document using the HTTP get method. In contrast, the unpublish operation is done through submission of a parameter embeded in the url with the HTTP post method. For this reason, there is no handling of XML in the code presented in this section. In a real application, one might want to adhere to one form of web service implementation rather than mix them as done here. However, we use both approaches in order to illustrate their differences. The differences will become apparent in subsequent sections when we complete the implementatins of the method stubs we use in the servlets in the wiki application.

The JSP

Figure 15.21 shows the contents of unpublish-page.jsp.

The Unpublish Page Servlet

Figure 15.22 shows the contents of UnpublishPageServlet.java.

252

```
package wiki.web;

import java.io.IOException;

import javax.servlet.RequestDispatcher;
import javax.servlet.ServletConfig;
import javax.servlet.ServletContext;
import javax.servlet.ServletException;
import javax.servlet.http.HttpServlet;
import javax.servlet.http.HttpServletRequest;
import javax.servlet.http.HttpServletResponse;

import org.apache.log4j.Logger;

import wiki.data.Page;
import wiki.data.PageDAO;

public class UnpublishPageServlet extends HttpServlet {
        private Logger logger = Logger.getLogger(this.getClass());

        private RequestDispatcher jsp;

        public void init(ServletConfig config) throws ServletException {
                ServletContext context = config.getServletContext();
                jsp = context.getRequestDispatcher("/WEB-INF/jsp/unpublish-page.jsp");
        }

        protected void doGet(HttpServletRequest req, HttpServletResponse resp)
                        throws ServletException, IOException {
                logger.debug("doGet()");
                String pathInfo = req.getPathInfo();
                String name = pathInfo.substring(1);
                Page page = new PageDAO().find(name);
                // Don't allow users to publish empty pages.
                if (page == null) {
                        resp.sendRedirect("../view/" + name);
                        return;
                }
                req.setAttribute("wikipage", page);
                jsp.forward(req, resp);
        }

        protected void doPost(HttpServletRequest req, HttpServletResponse resp)
                        throws ServletException, IOException {
                logger.debug("doPost()");
```

253

```
        // extract form data
        String pageName = req.getParameter("name");

        // Check for cancel button.
        String cancelButton = req.getParameter("cancel-button");
        if (cancelButton != null) {
                resp.sendRedirect("../view/" + pageName);
                return;
        }

        PageDAO pageDAO = new PageDAO();
        Page page = pageDAO.find(pageName);

        // Don't do anything if page doesn't exist or is already unpublished.
        if (page == null || !page.isPublished()) {
                resp.sendRedirect("../view/" + pageName);
                return;
        }

        // Invoke remote web service to unpublish page.
        logger.debug("invoking web service");
        unpublish(page);

        // Update page.
        page.setPublished(false);
        pageDAO.update(page);
        resp.sendRedirect("../view/" + page.getName());
    }

    private void unpublish(Page page)
    {
        // Implement later.
    }
}
```

Figure 15.22: UnpublishPageServlet

The doPost method invokes the publisher's web service inside the unpublish method, which we will implement at a later time.

254

```
<servlet>
   <servlet-name>unpublish-page</servlet-name>
   <servlet-class>wiki.web.UnpublishPageServlet</servlet-class>
</servlet>
<servlet-mapping>
   <servlet-name>unpublish-page</servlet-name>
   <url-pattern>/unpublish/*</url-pattern>
</servlet-mapping>
```

Figure 15.23: Deployment Descriptor

Deployment Descriptor

The following XML fragment needs to be added to the deployment descriptor to configure the unpublish servlet.

Test

Stop and start the wiki application with the manager application(**http://localhost:8080/manager/html/**). Then test the new functionality by starting at **http://localhost:8080/wiki/view/**. Try all possible combinations to verify that the application functions correctly. The unpublish confirmation page is shown in Figure 15.24.

Unpublish page

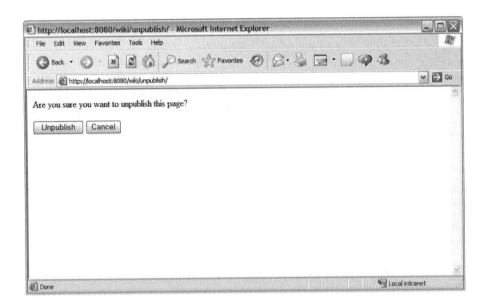

Figure 15.24: Unpublish Page

15.9 Exercises

(1) Confirming Cancelations :

When the user cancels the publish operation, he or she is brought back to the view page. The text mentioned that the user can verify that the operation was canceled by seeing the publish link in the view page as opposed to the unpublish link. Devise and implement a way to explicitly state to the user that the operation was cancelled.

(2) Exception Catching Filter :

Create and configure a filter to catch exceptions thrown in your code and make these exceptions appear in your log file. This makes it easier to see exceptions because you do not need to look into a different log file to see exceptions. To do this, do the following. Create a class called LogFilter that implements the javax.servlet.Filter interface. Add the following code to the doFilter method.

```
try {
    arg2.doFilter(arg0, arg1);
} catch (Exception e) {
    logger.error("", e);
    throw new ServletException(e);
}
```

Add the following code to web.xml.

```
<filter>
    <filter-name>log-filter</filter-name>
    <filter-class>wiki.web.LogFilter</filter-class>

</filter>
<filter-mapping>
    <filter-name>log-filter</filter-name>
    <url-pattern>/*</url-pattern>
</filter-mapping>
```

Test that exceptions are now written to your log file by introducing a bug into your code.

257

(3) Redirection :

Currently, requests for **http://localhost:8080/wiki/view**. Implement a redirection servlet that gets requests for **http://localhost:8080/wiki/view** and returns a redirection command to the browser to go to the following url.

```
http://localhost:8080/wiki/view/
```

Chapter 16

Web Services

16.1 Overview

There is no precise definition of a web service on which all agree. The meaning of the term sometimes depends on the context in which it used. For the purposes of this book, we define a Web Service as a software system that provides a programmatic interface over HTTP. Some people might add an additional restriction that the data exchanged between the client and server is formatted as XML documents. Still others might consider any short-lived application-to-application interaction over TCP to be a web service.

A common example of a web service is a payment processing service that is provided to commercial web sites. To understand how this works, imagine that a web application provides users with the ability to browse a catalog of items and place selected items into a shopping cart. At some point, the user decides to checkout. In a checkout page the application collects the credit card details from the user. When the user submits these credit card details to the application, the application makes a connection to a payment processing service and submits a request to charge the user's account with the amount he or she has agreed to pay for the items in the shopping cart. The payment processing service returns a result that indicates whether the payment has succeeded or failed. Typically, the messages sent between a web application and a payment service are transported over HTTPS. In this case, the payment service is called a web service.

There are different ways of implementing a web service. One method is to use the SOAP protocol in which XML data is placed inside a SOAP message and transported using HTTP. This approach is referred to as SOAP-based web services and is

259

a method being strongly supported by Microsoft and other large companies. There is a multitude of web service specifications related to SOAP-based web services. Many developers choose to avoid using the SOAP protocol, claiming that its complexity is unnecessary in many or most application contexts.

Another method of implementing web services is to place data in XML documents and transfer them directly using HTTP. This approach is commonly referred to as REST-based web services, although the term REST is also used to refer to an architectural style for implementing distributed systems. REST stands for Representational State Transfer. REST-based web services are much simpler to understand and implement than SOAP-based services. In this book, we illustrate the REST-based web services.

In this chapter we build functionality into the publisher and wiki applications that allows the wiki application to be a web service client of the publisher application. Specifically, when the user of the wiki application wishes to publish a given web page as an item in the publisher news feed, the wiki application will submit a publish request to the publisher application. To remove the web page from the publisher's news feed, the wiki application submits an unpublish request.

The server side implementation of our 2 web services are done using servlets, so that management of sockets and sending of HTTP headers are performed by the web container. In contrast, the client side implementation that we provide shows the details of creating a socket and sending HTTP message headers to the service. In many cases, application developers can avoid the direct use sockets, and the direct manipulation of HTTP headers. However, these developers need to be aware of the HTTP protocol and need to write code that reads, adds or modifies HTTP headers on occassion.

In this chapter we extend the publisher application by adding a REST-based interface that lets clients publish news items to its RSS feed. Specifically, we add 2 web services to the publisher application: one that allows clients to publish a news item through its news feed and another that allows clients to unpublish news items (remove news items from the RSS news feed). Also in this chapter, we complete the implementation of the publish and unpublish operations that users of the wiki application can invoke so that users of the wiki application can publish and unpublish wiki pages to and from the RSS news feed of the publisher application. Figure 16.1 illustrates the interactions between the various systems and their sub-components.

The stick figures above represent human access to the systems via browsers. When users of the wiki application invoke the publish operation on a given wiki page, the wiki application composes an XML document to serve as a web service request message

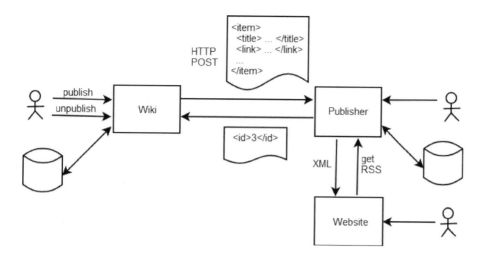

Figure 16.1: System Interactions

and sends this message to the publish web service of the publisher application. The request message contains the link to the wiki page and the wiki page title. The publisher application generates a unique id to represent the new news item, and then adds this id, the link and title information to its database. The publisher application then places the id in a simple XML document to be used for a web service response message, which it returns to the wiki application. The wiki application saves the returned id in its record for the wiki page being published. This returned id can be used later to unpublish (or delete) the wiki page from the RSS news feed.

After a wiki page is published in the manner just described, users visiting the home page of the website application will see the linkable title of the wiki page. This is accomplished in the HomeServlet of the website application, which retrieves the RSS document from the publisher application.

If the website were to be a high volume destination, requesting the RSS news feed for each request fot the website home page would result in too many redundant requests for the publisher's news feed. In this case, the developer could cache the RSS document and construct its home page from the cache in order to reduce this outgoing traffic and reliance on the publisher site. There are many ways to implement this improvement. The website could rely on a simple periodic check in which it requests the fresh version of the RSS document. Another possibility is for the website to register itself as a downstream client of the publisher's news feed and wait for the publisher to deliver to it revisions to the RSS document. In this situation, we say that the publisher pushes content to its clients. The RSS 2.0 protocol provides a means to accomplish this push mechanism.

16.2　A Web Service to Publish News Items

In this section we add a servlet to the publisher application that will enable connecting clients to add news items to the publisher application's news feed.

Create a new package in the publisher project called *publisher.ws* and create a publish news item service servlet in this new package with the implementation in figure 16.2.

```
package publisher.ws;

import java.io.BufferedReader;
import java.io.IOException;
import java.io.OutputStream;
import java.io.StringWriter;

import javax.servlet.ServletException;
import javax.servlet.http.HttpServlet;
import javax.servlet.http.HttpServletRequest;
import javax.servlet.http.HttpServletResponse;

import org.apache.log4j.Logger;
import org.jdom.Document;
import org.jdom.Element;
import org.jdom.JDOMException;
import org.jdom.input.SAXBuilder;
import org.jdom.output.XMLOutputter;

import publisher.data.NewsItem;
import publisher.data.NewsItemDAO;

public class PublishNewsItemService extends HttpServlet {
    private Logger logger = Logger.getLogger(this.getClass());

    protected void doPost(HttpServletRequest req, HttpServletResponse resp)
    throws ServletException, IOException {
        logger.debug("doPost()");

        // Read the XML request document.
        BufferedReader br = req.getReader();
        SAXBuilder builder = new SAXBuilder();
        Document requestDocument = null;
        try
        {
            requestDocument = builder.build(br);
```

263

```
    } catch (JDOMException e) {
       throw new RuntimeException(e);
    }

    // Extract title and link from request.
    Element item = requestDocument.getRootElement();
    Element titleElement = item.getChild("title");
    String title = titleElement.getText();
    Element linkElement = item.getChild("link");
    String link = linkElement.getText();

    // Create a news item from submitted data.
    NewsItem newsItem = new NewsItem();
    newsItem.setTitle(title);
    newsItem.setUrl(link);
    new NewsItemDAO().create(newsItem);

    // Create response document with id of newly
    // created news item.
    Element idElement = new Element("id");
    idElement.addContent(newsItem.getId().toString());
    Document responseDocument = new Document(idElement);
    StringWriter sw = new StringWriter();
    XMLOutputter outputter = new XMLOutputter();
    outputter.output(responseDocument, sw);
    String responseDocumentString = sw.toString();

    // Return response document.
    byte[] responseBytes = responseDocumentString.getBytes("UTF-8");
    resp.setContentLength(responseBytes.length);
    resp.setContentType("text/xml");
    OutputStream os = resp.getOutputStream();
    os.write(responseBytes);
    os.flush();
  }
}
```

Figure 16.2: class PublishNewsItemService

Observe that the publish servlet implements the doPost method and does not
implement the doGet method. This means that clients of the publish web service
will submit requests using HTTP POST messages, which means they will submit
news item data in the body of the HTTP request messages. We will follow the most

264

common convention, which is to structure the submitted data as an XML document. An example XML document that the client will submit is as follows.

```
<item>
   <title>Yahoo home page</title>
   <link>http://yahoo.com/</link>
</item>
```

When the doPost method is called, we extract the XML data with the SAXBuilder of the JDOM library. This is done with the following code.

```
// Read the XML request document.
BufferedReader br = req.getReader();
SAXBuilder builder = new SAXBuilder();
Document requestDocument = null;
try
{
   requestDocument = builder.build(br);
} catch (JDOMException e) {
   throw new RuntimeException(e);
}
```

The builder takes as an argument a BufferedReader, which provides access to the character data coming in from the client. The builder creates an object representation of the XML document and returns a reference to this object, which is of type Document. The build method of the builder object extracts the data from the buffered reader passed into it and constructs the document object. This operation relies on extracting data from an underlying communications socket, which may fail if there is a network or other communications error. The build operation may also fail if the incoming characters can not be parsed as an XML document. For these reasons, the build operation throws a checked exception that we handled with a try-catch block.

After the SAX builder builds an object representation of the submitted data in the form of an instance of the document class, we extract the title and link strings for the news item. To do this, we first obtain a reference to the root element of the request document, and then we access the children of the root elememnt, which are the title and link elements.

```
// Extract title and link from request.
Element item = requestDocument.getRootElement();
```

265

```
Element titleElement = item.getChild("title");
String title = titleElement.getText();
Element linkElement = item.getChild("link");
String link = linkElement.getText();
```

After we have the title and link for the news item, we use it to create an instance of the NewsItem class. This news item instance is passed into the create method of the newsItemDAO in order to store the news item data in the database.

```
// Create a news item from submitted data.
NewsItem newsItem = new NewsItem();
newsItem.setTitle(title);
newsItem.setUrl(link);
new NewsItemDAO().create(newsItem);
```

The create method has a side effect of creating and setting the id of the news item. The client needs this id in order to remove the news item from the RSS feed at some point in the future. For this reason, we return the id of the newly created news item to the client.

To return the news item id to the client, we follow the convention that data be exchanged within XML documents. The following XML document is an example of what we would return to the client, assuming that the id of the newly created news item is 3.

```
<?xml version="1.0" encoding="utf-8"?>
<id>3</id>
```

It is possible to create this XML document simply with the following code.

```
String responseDocString =
        "<?xml version=\"1.0\" encoding=\"utf-8\"?>" +
"<id>" + newsItem.getId() + "</id>";
```

However, we use JDOM library to create the XML response document in order to provide more consistency in the code and because it provides us with a better foundation to create more complicated documents in the future. The following code is resposible for contructing the XML document comprising the response from the server.

```
// Create response document with id of newly
// created news item.
Element idElement = new Element("id");
idElement.addContent(newsItem.getId().toString());
Document responseDocument = new Document(idElement);
StringWriter sw = new StringWriter();
XMLOutputter outputter = new XMLOutputter();
outputter.output(responseDocument, sw);
String responseDocumentString = sw.toString();
```

In the above, we construct an instance of the element class to represent the id element that will contain the string representation of the id we created for the news item. Because XML documents must have root elements, the contructor of the document class naturally takes an element in its contructor. This is the reason we pass the id element to the constructor of the document class to create the object the represents our response. We then use the XML outputter class to serialize the XML document into a string. It is this string that we will return to the client.

Finally, we return the response document to the client. When doing this, we need to pay attention to the encoding of the characters. The default character encoding for XML is UTF-8, which all XML parsers are required to support. For this reason, it is safest to return the XML document in the UTF-8 character encoding. The following code shows the process of returning the response to the client.

```
// Return response document.
byte[] responseBytes = responseDocumentString.getBytes("UTF-8");
resp.setContentLength(responseBytes.length);
resp.setContentType("text/xml");
OutputStream os = resp.getOutputStream();
os.write(responseBytes);
os.flush();
```

We start by invoking the getBytes method of the string representing the request document, passing into this method the argument UTF-8. This returns a byte array containing the raw binary representation of the message data. However, before we send the resulting bytes, we first set the HTTP content length and content type headers by calling the methods setContentLength and setContentType, respectively, on the response object. We then pass this byte array into the write method the output stream from the response object that was passed into our doPost method. When we

267

invoke the write command on the output stream in this way, Tomcat first sends the HTTP status line, followed by the response headers (including our content-length and content-type headers), followed by the bytes in the array. This sequence of actions is important to keep in mind when developing server-side logic; confusion on this point can be the source of incorrect logic.

Note that if we omit the content length header in the response, Tomcat will use the chunked encoding format to send the response document. In order to keep the client code simple, we avoid the chunked encoding format by setting the content length explicitly.

The following XML fragment needs to be added to the publisher's deployment descriptor to configure the publish servlet.

```
<servlet>
   <servlet-name>publish-service</servlet-name>
   <servlet-class>publisher.ws.PublishNewsItemService</servlet-class>
</servlet>
<servlet-mapping>
   <servlet-name>publish-service</servlet-name>
   <url-pattern>/publish</url-pattern>
</servlet-mapping>
```

Initially, we will allow all clients to invoke the web service; later we will require that clients authenticate to the server. To accomplish this, in the doFilter method of SecurityFilter, add the following lines of code to the correct place in order to allow unauthenticated clients to invoke the web service.

```
// Allow access to web service.
if (servletPath.equals("/publish"))
{
   chain.doFilter(req, resp);
   return;
}
```

At this point, we can not easily test the functionality of the publish web service because a test requires that an XML document be submitted to the publisher application, which is something that a web browser does not do when a form is submitted. (We could use JavaScript to do it using the XMLHttpRequest object.) In the next section, we will be able to test our implementation of the publish service by modifying the wiki application so that it invokes the service.

268

16.3 Invocation of the Publish Service from the Wiki Application

The code presented in this section relies on the JDOM library. You should copy the JDOM jar file from the publisher application into the WEB-INF/lib folder in the wiki application. Then, add the JDOM jar file to the build path of the wiki application.

In this section we modify the wiki application so that it calls the publish web service. Figure 16.3 contains the implementation of the helper method in the publish page servlet that calls to take care of the details of communicating with the publisher application. You should add this code to the publish page servlet of the wiki application. The publish method is declared as private because it will only be invokded from code inside the publish page servlet.

```
private String publish(Page page) throws IOException
{
   logger.debug("publish()");
   String pageName = page.getName();
   String pageUrl = "http://localhost:8080/wiki/view/" + pageName;

   SAXBuilder builder = new SAXBuilder();

   Element titleElement = new Element("title");
   titleElement.addContent(pageName);
   Element linkElement = new Element("link");
   linkElement.addContent(pageUrl);

   Element root = new Element("item");
   root.addContent(titleElement);
   root.addContent(linkElement);
   Document document = new Document(root);

   StringWriter sw = new StringWriter();
   XMLOutputter outputter = new XMLOutputter();
   outputter.output(document, sw);
   String docString = sw.toString();

   byte[] docBytes = docString.getBytes("UTF-8");
   String contentLengthHeader = "Content-length: " + docBytes.length + "\r\n";
   String contentTypeHeader = "Content-type: text/xml\r\n";
   String hostHeader = "Host: localhost\r\n";
   String connectionHeader = "Connection: close\r\n";
   String requestLine = "POST /publisher/publish HTTP/1.1\r\n";
```

269

```
Socket socket = new Socket("localhost", 8080);
OutputStream os = socket.getOutputStream();
os.write(requestLine.getBytes("US-ASCII"));
os.write(hostHeader.getBytes("US-ASCII"));
os.write(contentTypeHeader.getBytes("US-ASCII"));
os.write(contentLengthHeader.getBytes("US-ASCII"));
os.write(connectionHeader.getBytes("US-ASCII"));
os.write("\r\n".getBytes("US-ASCII"));
os.write(docBytes);
os.flush();

InputStream is = socket.getInputStream();
InputStreamReader isr = new InputStreamReader(is);
BufferedReader br = new BufferedReader(isr);

// Read through header lines.
while (true)
{
   String line = br.readLine();
   if (line.length() == 0) break;
}

Document responseDoc = null;
try
{
   responseDoc = builder.build(br);
} catch (JDOMException e) {
   throw new RuntimeException(e);
}

Element idElement = responseDoc.getRootElement();
String id = idElement.getText();
br.close();
return id;
}
```

Figure 16.3: helper method in the publish page servlet

When you organize imports on the above code, select the following classes from the lists presented to you.

- org.jdom.Document

270

- java.io.InputStream

- org.jdom.Element

- java.io.OutputStream

The publish method given above takes a wiki page object as its sole argument. It uses this object to construct a request to publish a news feed that points to the wiki page. To keep the example simple, we include only the title and wiki page link as data in the news feed. We start the implementation of the publish method by contructing variables that represent these two pieces of information: pageName and pageUrl.

The next thing we do is create an instance of SAXBuilder. SAX stands for simple API for XML. The SAX builder object is used for constructing XML documents. In our case, we use this object to construct the XML message to send to the publish service of the publisher application, which will contain the title and link for our wiki page.

Recall that the document that the wiki application submits to the publisher application contains a single root element called *item*, which represents the news item being submitted. The following XML document is an example.

```
<item>
    <title>Yahoo home page</title>
    <link>http://yahoo.com/</link>
</item>
```

Under the item element there are 2 children elements that contain text data (rather than sub-elements). The first child element is called *title*, and it contains within a start tag and an end tag the title of the news item. The second child element is called *link*, and it contains within a start tag and an end tag the url of the news article.

For each of the child elements, title and link, we create an instance of the JDOM element class. The following shows how we firts create the title element and then assign its contents. To keep the example application simple, we simply use the name of the wiki page for the title of the news item.

```
Element titleElement = new Element("title");
titleElement.addContent(pageName);
```

After creating the 2 child elements, we create an element to represent the root element item, and add the 2 child elements to it. This is shown in the following.

```
Element root = new Element("item");
root.addContent(titleElement);
root.addContent(linkElement);
```

We then create an instance of the JDOM document class to contain the root element as follows.

```
Document document = new Document(root);
```

We then create a StringWriter and an XMLOutputter. We pass the XML document and the string writer into the output method of the XML outputter class. The XML outputter writes a serialized version of the XML document into the string writer. We then extract the string that was written into the string writer and prepare to send this string to the publish service.

```
StringWriter sw = new StringWriter();
XMLOutputter outputter = new XMLOutputter();
outputter.output(document, sw);
String docString = sw.toString();
```

At this point, we have constructed a string that contains the MXL document to send to the service. We are going to write the character comprising this string into the output stream provided through a communication socket object. To prepare for this, we convert the string representation into a byte array as follows.

```
byte[] docBytes = docString.getBytes("UTF-8");
```

When converting characters into their byte equivalents, one must decide on a character representation. In our case, we use the UTF-8 representation, which is the default representation for XML documents.

The next set of operations is to construct the HTTP header that will precede the XML document in the outgoing stream of bytes.

272

```
String contentLengthHeader = "Content-length: " + docBytes.length + "\r\n";
String contentTypeHeader = "Content-type: text/xml\r\n";
String hostHeader = "Host: localhost\r\n";
String connectionHeader = "Connection: close\r\n";
String requestLine = "POST /publisher/publish HTTP/1.1\r\n";
```

The header of an HTTP/1.1 request message is comprised of a request line followed by 1 or more header lines. In our case, we send the content length, which is the number of bytes in the body of the request message. In our case, the content length is the number of bytes in the byte array representation of the XML document. We also send the content type, which is *text/xml*. The content type header specifies what is called the MIME-type of the object being transported in the body of the request message, which is a legacy term from the IETF email specifications. We send a host header that indicates the host name of the computer we are sending the message to. The host name header is the only request header that is required to be sent in version 1.1 of HTTP. The purpose of the host header is to inform the server which host name it resolved to get the server's IP address. This is useful in the case that a server has multiple host names (or virtual hosts). We send a connection header indicating that the underlying TCP connection will be closed by the client after the server returns a response. The request line is the the first line to be sent in an HTTP request. It starts with an HTTP method, POST in our case, followed by the name of a resource on the server, followed by the version of the HTTP protocol being used.

We then create a TCP socket connection to the server hosting the publisher application (localhost in our example) and send the HTTP request message to it.

```
Socket socket = new Socket("localhost", 8080);
OutputStream os = socket.getOutputStream();
os.write(requestLine.getBytes("US-ASCII"));
os.write(hostHeader.getBytes("US-ASCII"));
os.write(contentTypeHeader.getBytes("US-ASCII"));
os.write(contentLengthHeader.getBytes("US-ASCII"));
os.write(connectionHeader.getBytes("US-ASCII"));
os.write("\r\n".getBytes("US-ASCII"));
os.write(docBytes);
os.flush();
```

Note that Tomcat in our case is listening to port 8080. For this reason, Tomcat receives the HTTP message that we send (from inside Tomcat). Tomcat will parse the incoming HTTP message and construct an HTTPServletRequest object as a result. By examining the requested resource /publisher/publish, Tomcat determines to route the message to the publish servlet of the publisher application.

After sending the HTTP request message to the publisher application, it is time read the response message returned by the service.

```
InputStream is = socket.getInputStream();
InputStreamReader isr = new InputStreamReader(is);
BufferedReader br = new BufferedReader(isr);
```

We start by getting a reference to the input stream from the socket, which allows us to read raw bytes being returned to use through the TCP connection represented by the socket. We wrap the input stream in an input stream reader. This class converts the incoming stream of bytes into a stream of characters. The two streams mentioned so far do not do any buffering. We then wrap the input stream reader in a buffered reader, which allows us to read a line at a time. A line is a sequence of characters terminated by a new line character. Also, if the end of stream occurs, then the line can end this way as well.

We then enter a loop that reads through the header lines of the HTTP response message. HTTP header lines are terminated by an empty line, which is the condition we use to terminate the loop.

```
while (true)
{
    String line = br.readLine();
    if (line.length() == 0) break;
}
```

Once we are at the start of the HTTP message data, we are ready to parse the XML documment that the service is returning. We do this by calling the build method on the SAX builder object that we used at an earlier point to create the outgoing XML document.

```
Document responseDoc = null;
try
{
    responseDoc = builder.build(br);
```

274

```
} catch (JDOMException e) {
    throw new RuntimeException(e);
}
```

Recall that the document returned by the service looks like the following, minus any XML prolog (XML syntax preceding the root element).

```
{<id>3<id>}
```

Thus, once we have an object representing the XML document, we simply need to extract the text contents of its root element to obtain the id of the newly created news item.

```
Element idElement = responseDoc.getRootElement();
String id = idElement.getText();
br.close();
```

We then close the buffered reader, which closes the underlying input stream, and we return the extracted id to the calling code.

You should add the publish method to the publish page servlet of the wiki application and replace the code that in the doPost method that sets an artificial id with the id returned by a call to the publish method. Note that you must wrap the call to publish in a try-catch block because the publish method may throw an exception.

```
// Invoke remote web service to publish page.
try {
    String publishedId = publish(page);
} catch (Exception e) {
    logger.error(e);
    throw new RuntimeException(e);
}
```

Note that in this example code we do not handle communication failures or errors internal to the web service. In a real application, additional work would be needed to handle these failures.

Use the manager application(**http://localhost:8080/manager/html/**) to restart the wiki application. Then verify that all three applications – website, publisher and wiki – function as expected.

Open three different browser windows and point them to the following three pages.

- http://localhost:8080/wiki/view/hello

- https://localhost:8443/publisher/list-news-items

- http://localhost:8080/website/home

Click the publish operation on the hello wiki page. Refresh the list news items page to see the hello page appear in the list. Refresh the website page to see the new news item appear there as well.

16.4 The Unpublish Service

In this section, we add an unpublish service to the publisher application and we invoke this service from the wiki application when the user clicks on the unpublish link in a published wiki page.

We will implement the unpublish service differently than the publish service. In particular, we have the client send an HTTP GET request to the publisher application in order to unpublish a news item.

To remove a news item from the publisher's RSS feed, the client submits an HTTP GET request to the resource /publisher/unpublish. However, the publisher application also needs to know which news item in its database to delete. This is specified by an id parameter passed in as part of the resource specification. Thus, the full specification of the resource is in Figure 16.4 (assuming the id of the news item to remove is 3).

```
/publisher/unpublish?id=3
```

Create a new class in the publisher.ws package called UnpublishNewsItemService with the contents of Figure 16.4

```java
package publisher.ws;

import java.io.IOException;

import javax.servlet.ServletException;
import javax.servlet.http.HttpServlet;
import javax.servlet.http.HttpServletRequest;
import javax.servlet.http.HttpServletResponse;

import org.apache.log4j.Logger;

import publisher.data.NewsItem;
import publisher.data.NewsItemDAO;

public class UnpublishNewsItemService extends HttpServlet {
   private Logger logger = Logger.getLogger(this.getClass());

   protected void doGet(HttpServletRequest req, HttpServletResponse resp)
   throws ServletException, IOException {
     logger.debug("doGet()");
```

277

```
String id = req.getParameter("id");
NewsItemDAO newsItemDAO = new NewsItemDAO();
NewsItem newsItem = newsItemDAO.find(new Long(id));
if (newsItem != null)
{
    newsItemDAO.delete(newsItem);
}
    }
}
```

Figure 16.4: UnpublishNewsItemService

In the doGet method we obtain the id through a call to the getParameter method of the HttpServletRequest object, which is passed in as an argument to the doGet method. After obtaining the id, we perform two interactions with the news item DAO: we call find to obtain an instance of the NewsItem class that represents the news item we wish to delete, then we call the delete method of the news item DAO to delete the news item from the database. Note that we only call delete on the news item DAO if the news item was actually found because it is possible that another user has already deleted this news item from the database.

If we had designed the delete method of the news item DAO to take a news item id rather than an instance of the news item class, we would have been able to make a single call into the news item DAO rather than the 2 calls given in the above code. Two different people are likely to differ on their preferences for the form that the delete method takes. It may be that one form is better than the other. However, a more important issue is consistency in the DAOs; the code is easier to read and maintain when the delete methods of all DAOs follow the same pattern.

The following XML fragment should be used to the configure the newly created unpublish news item service.

```
<servlet>
    <servlet-name>unpublish-service</servlet-name>
    <servlet-class>publisher.ws.UnpublishNewsItemService</servlet-class>
</servlet>

<servlet-mapping>
    <servlet-name>unpublish-service</servlet-name>
    <url-pattern>/unpublish</url-pattern>
</servlet-mapping>
```

Recall that the security filter in the publisher application only allows unauthenticated requests for the login page and the news feed. We need to modify this filter in order to permit unauthenticated requests for servlet paths equals to */unpublish*. You can do this by adding the following code just after the code that checks for a match with /publish.

```
if (servletPath.equals("/unpublish"))
{
    chain.doFilter(req, resp);
    return;
}
```

Now, we need to modify the wiki application in order to invoke the unpublish web service when the user issues the command to unpublish a given wiki page. We prepared for this moment by defining a method stub (and unimplemented method) called unpublish in the unpublish page servlet. Figure 16.5 provides the implementation of the unpublish method; add this code to the unpublish page servlet of the wiki application.

```
private void unpublish(Page page)
throws IOException
{
    logger.debug("unpublish()");

    // Construct HTTP headers.
    String requestLine =
        "GET /publisher/unpublish?id=" +
        page.getPublishedId() +
        " HTTP/1.1\r\n";
    String hostHeader = "Host: localhost\r\n";
    String connectionHeader = "Connection: close\r\n";

    // Send HTTP headers.
    Socket socket = new Socket("localhost", 8080);
    OutputStream os = socket.getOutputStream();
    os.write(requestLine.getBytes("US-ASCII"));
    os.write(hostHeader.getBytes("US-ASCII"));
    os.write(connectionHeader.getBytes("US-ASCII"));
    os.write("\r\n".getBytes("US-ASCII"));
    os.flush();
```

279

```
// Read HTTP response.
InputStream is = socket.getInputStream();
InputStreamReader isr = new InputStreamReader(is);
BufferedReader br = new BufferedReader(isr);
while (true)
{
    String headerLine = br.readLine();
    if (headerLine.length() == 0) break;
}
}
```

Figure 16.5: unpublish method

Organize imports and select the following classes from the choices presented to you.

- java.io.InputStream

- java.io.OuputStream

The page object passed into the unpublish method represents the page that the client wishes to remove from the news feed. The only piece of information in this page object that we need is the news item id. This is what we need to send to the publisher application's unpublish service.

The following code shows how we construct the HTTP headers that comprise the HTTP request message that we will send to the publisher application.

```
// Construct HTTP headers.
String requestLine =
    "GET /publisher/unpublish?id=" +
    page.getPublishedId() +
    " HTTP/1.1\r\n";
String hostHeader = "Host: localhost\r\n";
String connectionHeader = "Connection: close\r\n";
```

The request line is the first line in an HTTP request message. It is comprised of 3 tokens: the HTTP method (GET in this case), the resource being requested (/publisher/unpublish?id="3" for example), and the protocol version number (HTTP/1.1).

280

The request line is where we use the news item id; this id is embedded in the resource token as the value of the id parameter.

The host header is a required in version 1.1 of HTTP, so we include this, although in our situation it has no effect other than to create a syntactically valid request message.

We include the connection close header so that the web service closes the TCP connection immediately after servicing the request. If we don't do this, the JDOM parser blocks on the input stream until the TCP connection times out. Therefore, we want the server to close the connection quickly, so that processing of the user request in the wiki application completes without delay.

After constructing the header strings we send them by making a socket connection with the server and writing the headers into the socket's output stream.

```
// Send HTTP headers.
Socket socket = new Socket("localhost", 8080);
OutputStream os = socket.getOutputStream();
os.write(requestLine.getBytes("US-ASCII"));
os.write(hostHeader.getBytes("US-ASCII"));
os.write(connectionHeader.getBytes("US-ASCII"));
os.write("\r\n".getBytes("US-ASCII"));
os.flush();
```

Unlike the XML documents that we send in the UTF-8 character encoding, we send the HTTP headers using the US-ASCII character encoding because it satisfies the HTTP protocol. All HTTP header lines are terminated by a carriage return and line feed sequence and the header section of HTTP messages is always terminated by a blank line. Therefore, the last header line we send is the string \r\n. After writing the headers, we flush the output stream to insure that the written bytes are pushed through any buffers and sent into the network.

The unpublish service is an example of one-way messaging because the client (wiki application) only sends a message to the service (publisher application) and does not read a response. However, the web service is implemented on top of HTTP, which is a request/response protocol. Therefore, the service will return an HTTP response message to the client. Rather than close the connection abruptly (and possibly generating an exception on the service end), we adhere to the HTTP protocol and read the HTTP response returned by the service.

```
// Read HTTP response.
InputStream is = socket.getInputStream();
InputStreamReader isr = new InputStreamReader(is);
BufferedReader br = new BufferedReader(isr);
while (true)
{
    String headerLine = br.readLine();
    if (headerLine.length() == 0) break;
}
```

The implementation of the unpublish method presented in this section does not handle abnormal events. One possible abnormal event is for an error to occur in the service. In this case, the service may return an HTTP error code, rather than a success code. In a more developed implementation, the HTTP response would be examined to see if such an error is reported from the service. In this situation, the wiki application may report the error to the user or handle it in some other way, such as to queue the unpublish request for a later attempt. An alternative to reporting errors in this way is to use 2-way messaging where the service returns a status code that reports a success or failure of the requested operation.

Test that the modifications you have just made are correct. To do this, use the manager application(**http://localhost:8080/manager/html/**) to stop and start the publisher application and to restart the wiki application. Open three different browser windows to point at the following three pages.

- **http://localhost:8080/wiki/view/hello**

- **https://localhost:8443/publisher/list-news-items**

- **http://localhost:8080/website/home**

Click the unpublish operation on the hello wiki page. Refresh the list news items page to see the hello page disappear in the list. Refresh the website page to see the new news item disappear there as well.

16.5 Security Mechanisms

Overview

In general, web services are made secure on the application level by satisfying the following criteria.

- The server and client authenticate (prove their identities) to each other.

- The communication channel is private. (Only the sever and client can read the exchanged messages.)

- Tampering of data by *a man in the middle* is detected.

Another application-level security property of interest for web services is *non-repudiation*, which enables the communicating end points to prove to third parties that they received messages from each other. Non-repudiation is accomplished through the use of digital signatures. We will not add this feature to the example applications.

In this section we show how to satisfy the 3 criteria given above in our example applications. Specifically, we will use Transport Layer Security (TLS), also referred to as Secure Sockets Layer (SSL), in which the server authenticates to the client through the use of the public key infrastructure (PKI). By using TLS/SSL in this way, the server will have authenticated to the client, the communication channel will be private, and tampering attacks will be detected. For client authentication, we will have the client present a secret access key with each request.

Public/Private Key Pair

The TLS/SSL protocol requires that the user posses a public/private keypair. The private key is keep a secret from everyone, but the public key is made public by distributing a public key certificate. In the case of web applications, the public key certificate contains the server's public key and identifying information for the server. The most important piece of identifying information in the certificate is the canonical name (CN), which is set to the host name of the application server. For example, the host name of the web server for California State University San Bernardino is *csusb.edu*. Also, the certificate is signed by a trusted entity whose self-signed certificate is held by connecting clients.

In our case, the certificate that our server will present to connecting clients is a self-signed certificate, Therefore, in order for clients to accept this certificate, we need to add the server's self-signed certificate to the client's container of trusted certificates called a *truststore*.

We already generated a self-signed certificate for the publisher application in the chapter on web application security. We did that with the following script, which runs under Windows.

```
keytool -genkey ^
        -keystore keystore ^
        -alias tomcat ^
        -keyalg RSA ^
        -keysize 2048 ^
        -dname CN=localhost ^
        -storepass changeit ^
        -keypass changeit
```

Notice that the canonical name is specified within the *distinguished name* (dname) parameter. To give an example of how the CN attribute is used by clients, consider the following. The client initiates a secure connection with a host with IP address that the DNS system returned for the domain name cnn.com. Initiating a secure connection means the client starts an SSL handshake procedure in which the server sends its certificate to the client. Suppose that the certificate presented to the server contained a CN value of csusb.edu. In this case, the client's secure socket subsystem rejects the connection because the CN value does not match with the host with which it is trying to connect. One way this could happen is if an attacker took control of the DNS server that the client uses to resolve domain names. We set the CN value to localhost because in our development environment, the client will connect to another process running on the same computer.

Create Truststore

Run the following command to extract the server's self-signed certificate from the keystore. Make sure you replace $TOMCAT_HOME with the path to tomcat on your system. Also, run the command in a terminal window with the current directory equal to the wiki folder within your Eclipse workspace. Note that the following command uses ^ for line continuation; for Linux and Mac, use \ instead.

```
keytool -export ^
        -rfc ^
```

```
-file publisher.cert ^
-alias tomcat ^
-storetype JKS ^
-storepass changeit ^
-keypass changeit ^
-keystore $TOMCAT_HOME/conf/keystore
```

You may need to try different forms of the above script to make it work on your system. For this purpose, it's convenient to place the command in a file, and run the file from the terminal window. For Windows, you could call the file extract_publisher_cert.bat, and for Linux/Mac, you can call it extract_publisher_cert.sh. I used the following to make the script run correctly on my system.

```
"C:\Program Files\Java\jre1.6.0_07\bin\keytool" ^
        -export ^
        -rfc ^
        -file publisher.cert ^
        -alias tomcat ^
        -storetype JKS ^
        -storepass changeit ^
        -keypass changeit ^
        -keystore "C:\Program Files\Apache Software Foundation\Tomcat 6.0\conf\keystore"
```

On successful completion of the command, it will report that it created the file publisher.cert. Check to see that this file exists in the wiki project folder in your Eclipse workspace.

The next step is to create a truststore that the wiki application will use for its secure connections. A truststore is a collection of trusted certificates. Run the following command from within the wiki project folder in your Eclipse workspace. If you are running under Linux or Mac, remember to replace ^ with \ for line continuation.

```
keytool -import ^
        -noprompt ^
        -alias tomcat ^
        -file publisher.cert ^
        -storetype JKS ^
        -keypass changeit ^
        -storepass changeit ^
        -keystore web/WEB-INF/truststore
```

Upon successful completion of the above command, a trust store file will be created in web/WEB-INF, which contains the certificate with the public key used by tomcat to establish TLS/SSL connections.

Modify Deployment Descriptor

We need to add an additional security constraint to the deployment descriptor of the publisher web application, so that requests for its 2 web services are redirected to the secure port. To do this, add the following security-constraint elements to the web-resource-collection element in the web.xml file.

```
<url-pattern>/publish</url-pattern>
<url-pattern>/unpublish</url-pattern>
```

These elements tell the Web container which URLs to apply the security restriction.

Add the following two lines to the contextInitialized2 method of the init class within the wiki application.

```
String trustStorePath = servletContext.getRealPath("/WEB-INF/truststore");
System.setProperty("javax.net.ssl.trustStore", trustStorePath);
```

In the wiki application, locate the following line inside the publish page servlet.

```
Socket socket = new Socket("localhost", 8080);
```

Replace this line with the following.

```
SocketFactory socketFactory = SSLSocketFactory.getDefault();
Socket socket = socketFactory.createSocket("localhost", 8443);
```

Perform the same replacement in the unpublish page servlet.

Start and stop the publisher and wiki applications, and verify that you can still publish and unpublish wiki pages.

286

Authenticating Clients

The next step is to add code needed for client authentication. There are many possible ways to do client authentication within the context of an SSL connection. The following are a list of some of the possible client authentication mechanisms.

1. Use HTTP basic authentication in which the username and password are base 64 encoded and included within a single header in each request.

2. Include the username and password in nonstandard (application defined) headers in every request.

3. Include username and password as elements in the XML document submitted to the service.

4. Require client authentication as part of SSL connection establishment.

5. Require a secret access key with each request.

In this section, we show how to add client authentication to the publisher web service by requiring that a secret access key be submitted by the client with each request. This is an authentication mechanism that is commonly used for REST-based web services.

Add the following code to the publish news item service. Place the code of the following listing just after the code that extracts the title and link from the request.

```
// Authenticate client.
Element accessKeyElement = item.getChild("accessKey");
if (accessKeyElement == null)
{
   resp.sendError(HttpServletResponse.SC_UNAUTHORIZED);
   return;
}
String accessKey = accessKeyElement.getText();
User user = new UserDAO().findByAccessKey(accessKey);
if (user == null)
{
   resp.sendError(HttpServletResponse.SC_UNAUTHORIZED);
   return;
}
```

Organize imports. Notice that the findByAccessKey method produces an error because it is not yet defined. Do the following instructions in order to learn a new way to conveniently add the findByAccessKey method to the UserDAO class.

Place the cursor in the string findByAccessKey. Hold down the control key and press 1. From the list choose Create method findByAccessKey(String) in type UserDAO.

Notice that the UserDAO file opens in the editor window and that a skeleton implementation of the findByAccessKey method is inserted in to the file. Replace the auto-generated contents of findByAccessKey with the contents of the following listing.

```
ResultSet rs = null;
PreparedStatement statement = null;
Connection connection = null;
try
{
    connection = getConnection();
    String sql = "select * from user where accesskey=?";
    statement = connection.prepareStatement(sql);
    statement.setString(1, accessKey);
    rs = statement.executeQuery();
    if (!rs.next())
    {
        return null;
    }
    return read(rs);
}
catch (SQLException e)
{
    throw new RuntimeException(e);
}
finally
{
    close(rs, statement, connection);
}
```

Modify the read method of UserDAO so that the access key is read from the database and written into the user object that it returns. The read method should look like the contents of the following listing when you are done.

```
private User read(ResultSet rs) throws SQLException
{
    Long id = new Long(rs.getLong("id"));
    String username = rs.getString("username");
    String password = rs.getString("password");
    String accessKey = rs.getString("accesskey");
    User user = new User();
    user.setId(id);
    user.setUsername(username);
    user.setPassword(password);
    user.setAccessKey(accessKey);
    return user;
}
```

Notice that the call to setAccessKey on the user object is marked by Eclipse as a compilation error. To fix this, you need to add an accessKey property to the user class. First, open the User class and declare a private member variable called accessKey of type String. Second, add the following accessor methods to the User class.

```
public String getAccessKey()
{
    return accessKey;
}
public void setAccessKey(String accessKey)
{
    this.accessKey = accessKey;
}
```

We need to add an accessKey column to the user table in the database. To do this, modify the createdb.sql script in the publisher project so that the user table creation command looks like the contents of the following listing.

```
create table user
(
    id integer primary key,
    username varchar(255) unique,
    password varchar(255),
    accesskey varchar(255) unique
);
```

The accesskey column needs to be unique so that an access key maps to a single user. Also, this declaration results in the construction of an index that makes the select command run efficiently when restricting the select to a given access key value using a select clause.

Modify the insertdb.sql script so that an access key is specified for the admin user. The following shows how the access key of 1234 is added to the insert command within insertdb.sql.

```
insert into user (id, username, password, accesskey)
values (4, 'admin', 'D033E22AE348AEB5660FC2140AEC35850C4DA997', '1234');
```

Run the all target of the ant build file so that tables are dropped, re-created and populated with sample data.

Now, we need to modify the unpublish service, so that it also checks for the access key. Add the following code to the doGet method of UnpublishNewsItemService. Place the code of the following listing before the code that looks up the news item to delete.

```
// Authenticate client.
String accessKey = req.getParameter("accessKey");
if (accessKey == null)
{
   resp.sendError(HttpServletResponse.SC_UNAUTHORIZED);
   return;
}
User user = new UserDAO().findByAccessKey(accessKey);
if (user == null)
{
   resp.sendError(HttpServletResponse.SC_UNAUTHORIZED);
   return;
}
```

Don't forget to organize imports.

Because we haven't modified the client in any way, client attempts to publish a news items should fail, since it is not currently programmed to send the access key.

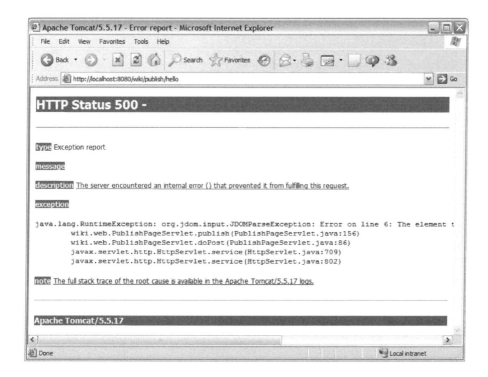

Figure 16.6: JDOM Parse Exception

Test

Stop and then start the publisher and wiki applications. Then try to publish a wiki page and verify that the operation fails and that the server reports a JDOMParseException as shown in Figure 16.6.

Actually, the publisher web service is returning a failure code through HTTP with the following line:

```
resp.sendError(HttpServletResponse.SC_UNAUTHORIZED);
```

The doPost method of the PublishPageServlet does not check for failure codes; it simply assumes that the request succeeded and then tries to parse the body of the response as an XML document with a single id element. Therefore, the wiki application reports a parse error, rather than a more useful error message. To fix this problem, read the HTTP status line separately from the request headers, and then after reading through the headers, check to see if the server returned a success code. The following lines of code show how this can be done in the publish method of the PublishPageServlet in the wiki application. The while(true) loop in the following snippet is already in the publish method; you need to add the line that reads the status line before this loop, and then add the code that checks for success after the loop.

```
// Read the HTTP status line (the first line of the HTTP headers in a response).
String statusLine = br.readLine();

// Read through the header lines.
while (true)
{
    String line = br.readLine();
    if (line.length() == 0) break;
}

// Check for success code.
if (!statusLine.startsWith("HTTP/1.1 200"))
{
    throw new RuntimeException("Publish web service failed with " + statusLine);
}
```

Now, restart the wiki application. Try to publish a wiki page and observe the more informative error message that is reported. Figure 16.7 shows the modified error message by updating the publish method.

Now, modify the publish method of PublishPageServlet so that the access key is sent with each request. Add the following two lines in the same place that we create the title and link elements.

```
Element accessKeyElement = new Element("accessKey");
accessKeyElement.addContent("1234");
```

Add the following line to the place in the code where we add titleElement and linkElement to the root element.

```
root.addContent(accessKeyElement);
```

292

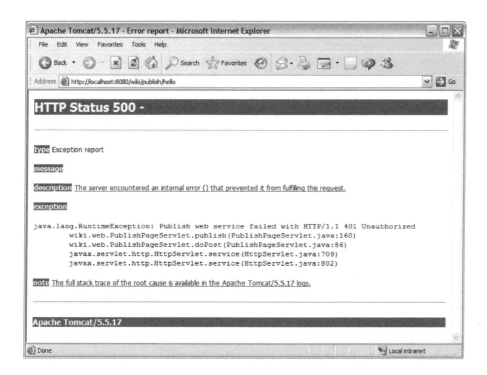

Figure 16.7: Modified Error Message For Publish Method

At this point, the wiki application is sending the access key with publish requests. We still need to have the wiki application send the access key with unpublish requests as well. To do this, modify the line in the unpublish page servlet that constructs the url request. The new line should look as follows.

```
String requestLine =
        "GET /publisher/unpublish?id=" +
        page.getPublishedId() +
        "&accessKey=1234 HTTP/1.1\r\n";
```

Restart the wiki application and try to publish and unpublish wiki pages. The applications should work correctly at this point.

16.6   Exercises

(1) Handling Failures :

The code presented in this chapter does not handle failures. For example, if the publisher application is not running, the wiki application will not be able to publish or unpublish news items. As presented, the code will in this case throw an exception, which gets reported to the user.

Modify the publish and unpublish servlets to gracefully handle the case that the publsiher application is either not running or is not reachable. In other words, instead of displaying the exception, display a message to the user that the service is currently not available and to try again later.

(2) News Item Quotas :

Modify the publisher application so that it limits the maximum number of news items that can be published by a given user. If a web service client (identified by an access key) tries to publish too many news items, inform the client that the news item failed to be created because the limit has been reached.

Modify the wiki application so that it reports failures to add news items because the quota has been reached.

Chapter 17

Conclusion

17.1 Overview

This book presented basic techniques of object-oriented design in Java web applications. This will help students to better understand object-oriented designs when they need to deal with them, and will also help the student to begin using object-oriented design in their own software creations. To improve your understanding of this area, you may want to study articles and books that cover design patterns.

This book adheres to the standard separation of application logic into model, view and controller that is found in most Java web applications, not to mention other language contexts, such as PHP and Ruby on Rails. The techinques are build on top of Servlets and JSPs, which is the starting point for more sophisticated approaches. After understanding the basic approach presented in this book, the student should be able to master MVC frameworks, such as Struts or Springframework, that are built on top of servlet and JSP.

The use of the DAO design pattern to hide the database and present a persistence service to the application has prepared you to begin a study of object relational mapping frameworks, such as Hibernate and Enterpise Java Beans, and understand how these are integrated into the web application.

Additional study should be devoted to application security.

Additional reading and study should be devoted to database topics, including transaction processing, crash recovery, and distributed databases. Although not mainstream, the student might look into object-oriented databases as an alternative to relational databases.

This book did not cover methods to scale web applications to handle loads that exceed the capacity of a single server. Because this is a typical situation in commercial web sites, the student should investigate techniques for distributing load across multiple servers.

Made in the USA
San Bernardino, CA
01 November 2013